ANALYTIXZ

20 *Years*

of

CONVERSATIONS AND ENTER-VIEWS

with

PUBLIC ENEMY'S
MINISTA OF INFORMATION

ANALYTIXZ

20 *Years*

of

CONVERSATIONS AND ENTER-VIEWS

with

PUBLIC ENEMY'S
MINISTA OF INFORMATION

PROFESSOR GRIFF

Heirz to the Shah Publishing

&

RATHSI
PUBLISHING

Website: WWW.RATHSIPUBLISHING.COM
Email: INFO@RATHSIPUBLISHING.COM

ATTENTION CORPORATIONS, UNIVERSITIES, COLLEGES AND PROFESSIONAL ORGANIZATIONS:
Quantity discounts are available on bulk purchases of this book for educational, gift purposes, or as premiums for increasing magazine subscriptions or renewals. Special books or book excerpts can also be created to fit specific needs. For information, please contact:

To book Professor Griff for any special event, including (but not limited to), a: conference, seminar, college campus, community group, book signing, lecture and/or as a consultant; please contact (678) 557-2919 or email professorgriff@hdqtrz.com.

Cover Photo by Keith Pegues; Cover Design by Keith of Marion Designs; Transcribing by Al 'Ade' Singleton & Deidra DS Green, Sis Latanya, Tyra Coles and Lisa Manley; Coordinating by: Jahi Muhammad and Patrick Muhammad; Technical Arrangements by: Khalil Amir

ISBN: 978-0-9771242-1-3

Library of Congress 2009934937

Dedication

"Dedication rewards those that are dedicated!"
-Dr Rev Phil Valentine

To my children

Taqiyyah K. Shah, Rasheem Khaliqq, Khalil Amir, Nailah Miasia and Isa Shah. My Granddaughter Lajoi Ali.

My family

To the Griffin family, the Simpson family and the Warner's (West Virginia)

To my extended family

Juanna Williams and family, Randy Glaude, Arlisha "Angel' Sims , Marcus "Society" Effinger, Jason Orr, Earle and Marilyn Holder, Kyle Jason and family, Meson Williams and Family, "The Earnsta" Ernest Grant and family. Benjamin Ransom and family, Tyra Coles and family

My GOD children

Abdul Azeem Ahmed Muhammad , Lakeshia Muhammad, Latif Bro Butch and Sonseare X (sonny Extra)
Malik Jamal Carter, Shawn Carter and Tamika Robinson Carter
Akaia Assata Simone Sokoni, Opio and Kafi Sokoni
Jazziman Francis, Rabiyah Karim-Kincey and Harmony Rutland.
(Miss R), Jade "Juana Williams", Isabel Belloso.

In loving memory of

Louis Griffin, James Simpson, Zasia Holder and
My sister Sophie Bashir (Marseilles, France).

Acknowledgements

To those who have advanced the cause of liberation for our people whom I had the pleasure of meeting with, soldiering with, know that you have touched me in a way I can't thank you enough, so I acknowledge you.

Master W.F. Muhammad, Elijah Muhammad and Minister Louis Farrakhan. The PE Family, Chuck D and Gaye, Bro Mike, pop diesel Bro John X Oliver, James "Bomb" Allen, new York city mike Michael Faulkner, My 7th octave band mate Khari Wynn, Brian Hardgroove, Greg Clifton Johnson, Flavor Flav and team flavor, The Drew , Johnny Juice, Keith Shockley, Sean Devore, Walter Leaphart, Latham Hodge and Dan Lugo, Gary G-whiz and family. Dr "Quo" Wetherspoon, my man "E" Eric Ridenhour, the badest Dj on the planet DJ LORD. Trinity and Abnormal. C-Doc the filmsta, Adam Wallenta, Black Dot, KB, Saa Neter, Queen Afua, Otim Larib, Phil Valentine, Llaila O. Afrika, Professor James Small and Professor Simmons ,Kamau and Mwesha Kambon, Ashra and Meri-ra Kwesi, Tuneseo Sanema, Shawn Muhammad. Mwalimu K. Bomani Baruti, Sister Ya, Nisa Shabazz, Christin Henry, Steve X, Kamia and Asha Mance, Shaheed M. Allah, Lisa Manley and family. Demetria "MiMi" Clark, Lashonda Pressley, Khalid El-Hakim Black History mobile museum, Ron Devoe (New Edition). Sam Sneed, Neal Kelley, Adel Mooney, Toni Fields, Sonia Evans, Dres the Beatnik, Sonja Muhammad. Mooney and Fuma, Debra Anderson and family, my west coast fam Jenaba, Sadiki Bakari, Kiedi Obi Awadu, Brother Jamal, Storm, Mr. and Mrs. Williams (Ya), "Martone", my big sister Marimba Ani. To those brothers who stood up in the face of the enemy to our people NY OIL, Immortal Technique and Dead Prez you give strength to Precise Science and brothers keepers each one teach three. To IRAS and Uno the Prophet Jahmahl Crawford keep doing the dam thing and to the baddest MC's on the planet KRS-ONE and WISE INTELLIGENT, Cannibus, Immortal Technique....peace.

DJ Earth One, Supa nova slum.

To all of those who donated to the survival of myself and my family during the time of my house fire thank you, thank you, thank you. Pam Africa, Mumia Abu Jamal, Sabrina Green, Kalonji Jama Changa and the FTP Movement. Ray Hagin's and the African Village family, Coach Powell, Dr. Kevin Washington, Dr. Wade Nobles, Mutana's, Lovin it Live, Blue Seas, Soul Veg and Calabash Vegetarian Ketchen Llaila Afrika, Dr. Scott Whitaker, Queen Afua for keeping us healthy. Nubian Bookstore, MEDU Bookstore, Sankofa in DC, Jaye Evans (Columbus, Ohio), Rashaan M. Robinson, Calvin Benjamin.

INTERVIEWS TO ENTER-VIEW TO INNER-VIEW
"interviews to enter my view to experience my inner view"

INTROView

About the Author

Professor Griff is an internationally renowned educator, writer, producer, musician, platinum recording/spoken word artist, lecturer and founding member of the pioneering and revolutionary hip hop group *Public Enemy*. Author of the popular music business guide: **Musick Bizness R.I.P. (Resource Information Publication),** Griff stands as a highly acclaimed, seasoned entertainment industry veteran and sought-after resource on all aspects of the music business.

An activist within both the conscious and hip hop communities, Griff currently stands as a permanent fixture on the international lecture circuit with his riveting and powerful discourse/book, the **"Psychological Covert War on Hip Hop."** An energetic and passionate educator, Griff skillfully customizes this extensively documented lecture to suit the needs of all audiences. Armed with an exemplary life of service and an impressive twenty-year musical career, Griff captivates audiences with his universal call for social responsibility within both the hip hop community and larger culture. As perhaps a testament to his firm commitment to raise the level of consciousness of today's entire hip hop generation; Griff effortlessly draws upon his own extensive entertainment industry experience and a vast reservoir of historical scholarship and research to deliver this poignant message.

Reared in Long Island, New York and a current resident of Atlanta, Georgia; Griff maintains a coveted role as Minister of Information for *Public Enemy* and is currently celebrating an unprecedented *'sixty'* world tours and 20th Year Anniversary, with the group. A well-rounded music enthusiast, Griff is also a member of the hip hop/metal band *7th Octave,* and has created an empowering youth hip hop curriculum entitled "Kidhoppaz," designed to fuse education and entertainment into a positive, effective instructional module.

Musically, Griff has recorded nine albums with his group Public Enemy however he has long distinguished himself as a talented and acclaimed solo artist as well. Namely, while signed to Luke Records Griff wrote, produced and recorded three powerful and thought-provoking albums entitled: "Pawns in the Game" (1990), "Kaoz II Wiz-7-Dome" (1991) and "Disturb N Tha Peace (1992)." Also, in 1998, Griff released "Blood of the Profit" on Lethal Records. With his group Confrontation Camp Griff recorded the album "Objects in the Mirror May be Closer than they Appear" (2000) and "The Word Became Flesh" (2001); with his group 7th Octave he recorded the album "The Seventh Degree (2004)." Griff has appeared in the following films: "Turntables" and "The Chip Factor," in addition he spearheaded the production of the informative documentary entitled "Turn off Channel Zero."

Griff holds a Bachelor of Science degree in Education, is a licensed personal security defense instructor, and an accomplished martial artist. An avid lecturer, known for his innate ability to impart life-changing ideas, concepts and techniques for the spiritual/personal growth and development of all who attend his lectures, Professor Griff is uniquely equipped to meet the needs of an international wide-ranging audience.

Remaining true to his title as Minister of Information, Professor Griff has continued his vigilance by providing information for the masses. Most recently, he has published the *Atlanta Musick Bizness Resource Information Publication* (R.I.P.) providing invaluable industry information for those interested in breaking into the business of MuSick.

Griff's current projects include: 7th Octave- God Damage Album; Psychological Covert War on Hip-Hop (book & lecture); Metaphysical Goddestry of the Soul of Hip-Hop (book & lecture) and more in the works.

1 Corinthians 13:11 When I was a child, I spoke like a child, thought like a child, and reasoned like a child. When I became a man, I gave up my childish ways.

ON THE RECORD
Setting the Jewish Question Straight
Sister Rah and Professor Griff
Interview August 6th, 2009

SR: This is Sister Rah and I am sitting with Professor Griff of Public Enemy and we are interviewing for the book "Analytixz" we want to talk about what initially sparked the controversy surrounding supposed anti-semetic sentiments from Professor Griff during the early years of Public Enemy circa 1989. So, Professor Griff, what is anti-Semitism?

PG: I think before we answer that question, we need to let the people know this is, how many years later?

SR: About 20 years later.

PG: But this is the mindset that I had back then. So I want people to use this mindset as a back drop into the thinking I had at that time.

PG: Wow! This is 2009, August 6th? So you are talking 20 some odd years the whole negative energy of that particular interview, and that interview still affects people's lives. Yes, we need to let the people know the whole time frame, the time that has lapsed and it affects every aspect of my life personally and I guess those people that were involved, especially the careers and lives of those in Public Enemy,

1

and those that may be listening to this or reading this should keep that in mind.

PG: Anti-Semitism, as told to us and taught to us by the Most Honorable Elijah Muhammad.

Malcolm was called anti-Semite, and other people way before Professor Griff was called anti-Semite and accused of making anti-Semitic statements. If properly defined I think the people would understand.

First of all it is impossible for a black man to be anti-Semitic. We were given the question by the Most Honorable Elijah Muhammad in our lessons the supreme wisdom "Who is the original man?," and the answer is the original man is the Asiatic Black man, the maker, the owner, the cream of the planet earth, God of the universe. If we are the Fathers and Mothers of everyone on the planet, and when you follow the chronology not only of history, if you look into history and find who the Semitic people were and the Semitic languages in the particular land area or geographical location on the planet, you will find that we were black people. And we were the Semitic people in that land. In order for me to be anti-Semitic, I would have to be anti-self, Anti-black, which is impossible. Now, the people that came down out of the Caucus Mountains they have taken this term "Semitic" to relate to who they are as a people, and that's not correct. You can read Michael Bradley's book, "People of the Caucus," deeper than that you can go on-line and listen to Tim Wise who talks about the history of the white race and the power and privilege. These are the people who stole the Blackmans history and put their name on it. Read Chancellor Williams book "Destruction of Black civilization." We could debate that all day long, but history will show and prove that they are not the Semitic people, that we are the Semitic people. I would have to be anti-self, anti the original Arab, anti original Japanese, anti original Chinese, anti original everybody on the planet in order for me to be anti-Semitic. But, they have taken this term, anti, meaning against, and put it before this term Semitic and used anti-Semitic as a rallying cry to galvanize that energy to come against anyone who's anti their theft of our history, we are the original Hebrews we are the original Jews. We are not necessarily anti them as a people. They have a right to exist. All the other people on the planet come from Black people and we are all part of the human family. But to use that as a rallying cry simply because someone disagrees with your ideology and philosophy is a whole different story.

Anti-Semitic - *A person who is against any cultural or faith based group of people, not just Jewish people. Hitler was anti-semitic to Jews, gypsies and Russians. The act of hatred towards Jewish people; a person who is against the Jewish faith or against Jews in general.*

SR: Okay. So according to what most people think in terms of Semetic, what is a Semite?

PG: According to what most people think, a Semite is someone that's from the "Semitic" languages and people; this does not include white people from the caucus mountains. This includes those of Jewish origin, the Hebrew origin, or any of those families that are related to the whole Jewish experience, (i.e.) Jewish religion, Jewish people, Jewish experience. So when we think of the Semitic people we think of everyone in that particular bloodline. But this is not what it really is.........

Semitic - *In linguistics and ethnology, Semitic (from the Biblical "Shem") was first used to refer to a language family of largely Middle Eastern origin, now called the Semitic languages. This family includes the ancient and modern forms of Akkadian, Amharic, Arabic, Aramaic, Ge'ez, Hebrew, Maltese, Phoenician, Tigre and Tigrinya among others. As language studies are interwoven with cultural studies, the term also came to describe the extended cultures and ethnicities, as well as the history of these varied peoples as associated by close geographic and linguistic distribution. The concept of "Semitic" peoples is derived from Biblical accounts of the origins of the cultures known to the ancient Hebrews. Those closest to them in culture and language were generally deemed to be descended from their forefather Shem. Enemies were often said to be descendants of his cursed nephew, Canaan. In Genesis 10:21-31, Shem is described as the father of Aram, Asshur, and Arpachshad: the Biblical ancestors of the Arabs, Aramaeans, Assyrians, Babylonians, Chaldeans, Sabaeans, and Hebrews, etc., all of whose* *languages are closely related; the language family containing them was therefore named Semitic by linguists. However, the Canaanites and Amorites also spoke a language belonging to this family, and are therefore also termed Semitic in linguistics, despite being described in Genesis as sons of Ham (See Sons of Noah). Shem is also described in Genesis as the father of Elam and Lud, although the Elamites and Lydians usually thought to descend from these spoke languages that were not Semitic.*

Semite - *The term Semite means a member of any of various ancient and modern people originating in southwestern Asia, including Akkadians, Canaanites, Phoenicians, Hebrews, Arabs, and Ethiopian Semites. It was proposed at first to refer to the languages related to Hebrew by Ludwig Schlözer, in Eichhorn's "Repertorium", vol. VIII (Leipzig, 1781), p. 161. Through Eichhorn the name then came into general usage (cf. his "Einleitung in das Alte Testament" (Leipzig, 1787), I, p. 45). In his "Gesch. der neuen Sprachenkunde", pt. I (Göttingen, 1807) it had already become a fixed technical term.[1] The word "Semitic" is an adjective derived from Shem, one of the three sons of Noah in the Bible (Genesis 5.32, 6.10, 10.21), or more precisely from the Greek derivative of that name, namely Σημ (Sēm); the noun form referring to a person is Semite.*

Semitic languages - *Branch of the Hamito-Semitic language; see Afro-Asiatic language.*

Afro-Asiatic language - *Any of a family of languages spoken throughout the world. There are two main branches, the languages of North Africa and the languages originating in Syria, Mesopotamia, Palestine, and Arabia, but now found from Morocco in the west to the Gulf in the east. The North African languages include ancient Egyptian, Coptic, and Berber, while the Asiatic languages include the largest number of speakers – modern Arabic – as well as Hebrew, Aramaic, and Syriac. The scripts of Arabic and Hebrew are written from right to left.*

SR: Okay.

PG: That is what the average person thinks, they don't think Black. They don't think that we are the original Hebrews. They don't think that way at all.

SR: So is there a difference between the identifications of Jew and Jewish?

PG: Oh yes.

SR: Can you explain?

4

PG: I think when you ask someone that is a Jew, so to speak, a lot of them need to be taught. They will tell you, and even get confused in how they answer it, that a Jewish person is a part of the Jewish religion, which we beg to differ, because what is the Jewish religion? Where can we find this particular religion? If the Jewish religion derives from Judah, from the scriptures, then we know where that origin comes from and we can easily follow that blood line right on back to Black people. If the individual called Judah even existed. So, in dealing with it from a religious context, of course we can differentiate, even when we go among them.

We may not differentiate between Jewish and Jew when you come among black people because we don't have a definition of what a Jew is or what Jewish is. Now, I discarded this concept called religion all together. This interview took place in '89, this is 2009, to have that argument we would spend the next two or three days having that discussion about what terms meant in '89 as opposed to 2,000 years ago and as opposed to 2009. Those definitions have changed, they have even broadened and changed the definition of anti-Semite since Minister Farrakhan, Ice Cube, Dr. Khalid, Leonard Jefferies, Professor Griff, Tony Martin, I could go on and on and on. All of us were labeled anti-Semite. And even recently, with Steve Cokely. So, for me to give you a definition in 2009, hell, by the time this comes out it may change. (Laughter)

Jew - *An ethnoreligious group originating in the Israelites or Hebrews of the Ancient Near East. The Jewish ethnicity, nationality, and religion are strongly interrelated, as Judaism is the traditional faith of the Jewish nation*

Jewish - *"Who is a Jew?" is a basic question about Jewish identity. The question has gained particular prominence in connection with several high-profile legal cases in Israel since the founding of the Jewish state in 1948. The definition of who is a Jew varies according to whether it is being considered by Jews for self-identification or by non-Jews for their own particular purposes. As Jewish identity can include characteristics of an ethnicity and of a religion, the definition of who is a Jew has varied, depending on whether a religious, sociological, or ethnic aspect was being considered. This article is concerned with Jewish self-identification issues.*

Hebrew - *Hebrew ('Ivrit) is a Semitic language of the Afro-Asiatic language family. Hebrew in its modern form is spoken by more than seven million people in Israel while Classical Hebrew has been used for prayer or study in Jewish communities around the world for over two millennia. It is one of the official languages of Israel, along with Arabic. Ancient Hebrew is also the liturgical tongue of the Samaritans, while modern Hebrew or Palestinian Arabic is their vernacular, though today about 700 Samaritans remain. As a foreign language it is studied mostly by Jews and students of Judaism and Israel, archaeologists and linguists specializing in the Middle East and its civilizations, by theologians, and in Christian seminaries. The modern word "Hebrew" is derived from the word "ivri" which in turn may be based upon the root "`avar" meaning "to cross over". The related name Ever occurs in Genesis 10:21 and possibly means "the one who traverses". In the Bible "Hebrew" is called Yehudith because Judah (Yehuda) was the surviving kingdom at the time of the quotation, late 8th century BCE (Is 36, 2 Kings 18). In Isaiah 19:18, it is also called the "Language of Canaan".*

SR: Okay. To shift gears a little bit, how long have you been affiliated with the group, Public Enemy?

PG: I haven't been affiliated. I am Public Enemy. Since the out start, since its conception, Professor Griff has been there. So, to associate myself with an entity that I am, is ridiculous.

SR: Okay so you were a founding member of the group?

PG: Yes, of course. When we got together, we discussed the look, the ideology, the philosophy and what we would do. Yes, I was there from the out start. My private conversations with Chuck D and Hank Shockley of the Bomb Squad, those conversations that no one was privy to but us three. We knew what the plan was. Chuck D and Hank Shockley was one of the ones that sat with me and I sat with them and we laid out what the plan would be. That plan did not include this, the controversy we speak of today. Elijah Muhammad taught us that the white man is so insignificant we would have to tie a string around our finger to remind us that he even exists.

SR: What was your role in the group?

6

PG: From the out start, Minister of Information, gathering of information for what the songs would consist of, not to take anything away from what Chuck and Hank have ever done, because I leave all the genius to them when it comes to that final product, what the public actually heard. I was road manager, because they said they needed someone competent and responsible to keep track of the money, to keep things in order. I was leader of the S1W's, and that security force not only on stage but off stage, and even on the spiritual realm. And Chuck D will tell you that we would define S1W as those individuals that secured the fact that we are First World people, and not Third World people. So I had four or five different roles.

SR: The many reports at the time said that you were the "self proclaimed" Minister of Information. Is this true, or were you agreed upon by the group to be Minister of Information?

PG: Definitely not self appointed. Definitely not self-proclaimed. That was a title bestowed upon me by Chuck D; so we would have to ask him that question. But us being students of the Black Panther Party History, we borrowed that title from the Black Panther Party. The look, title, energy is what we were talking about, mainly information from Islam philosophy, rhetoric and teachings, Black Panther Party, Mau-Mau wherever we can get it from.

SR: As the Minister of Information were you considered the spokesperson for the group?

PG: Yes, for a period of time I was the spokesperson for the group, and knowing that this mission would only last for two years I felt that sense of urgency. So, if people would keep that in mind I think they would understand the context in which not only the Jewish question, the whole anti-White, the whole pro-Black...where that mindset and that energy and spirit was coming from and the bed that was made and the atmosphere created around it.

SR: So now you just mentioned two years appointed for the mission, could you explain that further?

PG: It was proposed to me by Chuck D himself that the whole Public Enemy mission would last for two years. That we would get in, shock the industry with what we had to say, raise the conscious level of our people and get out.

SR: Why two years?

PG: I think, from a personal note, we've often talked about us being dead, in jail; we have often talked about that it would only last two years. They would only allow us to do this for two years. They, meaning the white power structure who've murdered and jailed every black leader to ever speak for our cause, that kind of talk. "You better hurry up and say what you have to say now because in two years it is going to be over and done." We wouldn't even be around to see what we are seeing today. To see what we were saying, what we were doing, how it would affect the people today. We wouldn't even be around. This was coming from Chuck D himself. So that is why in our music, the urgency. You've heard "Bring the Noise?" It was like, "Man, we ought to do this now."

SR: Why were you selected for the position, Minister of Information?

PG: Growing up with Chuck in those early days (Laughter), those early days when I had a crew of about 107 deep. Rolling up into parties. You see, I have this kind of reputation which I really don't want to talk about (Laughter). I think I was chosen because I was a studious individual. I went to Nassau Community College for two weeks so I was prepared for this job. (Laughter). In the Nation of Islam at the behest of my brother Anwar (Ronald X) and my brother Michael

X, there I just came through the ranks of Islam, being very studious. I guess Chuck saw in me...this brother can not only be a leader of the S1W's and road manager, the information that this brother has you know, we need to make this stuff into songs.

SR: So, this was something you were into long before the inception of Public Enemy?

PG: Way before Public Enemy. Me and Hank Shockley had hooked up on the music tip way before Chuck D. So, with that known by the people, it's like, "You were already doing music with the Bomb Squad in Spectrum City." You were already doing the parties and securing the parties, you were already dropping knowledge up in the parties on the microphone. I was already there. I was already doing these things, so this kind of stuff was nothing new to me.

SR: So how active were you in developing the so called message of Public Enemy?

PG: I think it wasn't left in my hands; it had to be put in the spirit and frequency of Hip-Hop. I think that is where the genius of Chuck D comes in because if you are talking about, I am giving you video cassettes and cassette tapes and manuscripts and documents, books, you have got to turn that into a 3 and ½ minute song and it takes a high form of alchemy to do that. Like when you hear Slick Rick, Doug E. Fresh and Dana Dane telling those particular stories that they told, Just Ice and other people that told the story it's like ...wow! Ice Cube, when he told the story of what happened to him in just one day Xzibit and other people...it's like okay, we have to take that and morph it into a 3 minute song. Although, this may have happened to us in the course of 24 hours, we've got to condense that into a 3 minute song and keep it on beat, with rhythm and entertaining. So, I think that is the form of alchemy we had to use and use that Hip-Hop frequency to turn it into something that you could nod your head to, dance to, and get your soul moving, and stirring. So

9

much so it would be nothing to talk revolution into the head and hearts of your people. When you say instrumental, in putting songs together, sitting next to someone writing every note, no, being there every night in the studio, no. Intense conversations, arguing, building as we use to say "Standing in Cyphers." That is how it came about.

SR: **Okay, so while Chuck D. was the front man your influence could still be heard in the lyrics as the collective that was known as Public Enemy?**

PG: Right and you look at Public Enemy and listen to what we are saying and you've seen the visual okay, you can say, "Yes, I can see Griff's influence."

SR: **Now, 22 years later Public Enemy actually came into the music industry in what 1987, '86?**

PG: '87.
SR: Okay.

PG: Even before that, when Jam Master J had personal conversations with Chuck. When DMC had those personal conversations and Bill Stephaney and Chuck D., at Adelphi University, being the D.J. So the whole idea of Public Enemy was forming. Did we know that we were going to call it Public Enemy because it was really, Chucky D.? It wasn't even Chuck and Flava then, it was Chucky D. that Rick, Rick really wanted to sign Chuck to a contract. Chucky D. coming out of Spectrum City with Hank Shockley being out at Adelphi, Bill Stephanie, Harry Allen, and Keith Shockley, that whole crew coming from Long Island. So, it was the Chucky D. Show. Then it was the Chuck and Flava thing, and then it morphed into Griff and Terminator then I brought the S1W's and then it morphed into Chuck creating, coming up with the name with the logo, since he graduated from Adelphi University graphic design and it morphed into something beautiful.

10

SR: So, now of course, 20 years later, 2009, as best as you can recall what did you say during the interview in London that sparked all the anti-Semitic controversy?

PG: As best as I can recall, and I am not, as we say on the street quote unquote 'punking out,' as best as I can recall sitting with Andreas 13X. I am sitting across from a very light skinned, fair skinned brother David Mills for about an hour and twenty minutes, probably longer than that. We are talking about music, we were talking about who controlled the music industry and then the conversation gets deeper and we started to talk about the <u>International Jew</u>, written by Henry Ford. I started to talk about Steve Cokely and the information he has brought forth in reference to Jewish history and the Jewish question. I mentioned the book called <u>The Octopus</u>, I forget the author; this is best as I can recall. Rolling my mind back on that day, I remember having tension with S1W's and Chuck because he was having tension with Hank Shockley and some other people about some other issues and he was blowing me off and I'm setting up the interviews, there are people in the lobby waiting, and I see him and I'm like "...you know we have some people waiting." He said "Man, the hell with that, you handle it. You go do interviews; I don't feel like doing anything." Wow, I'm setting up these interviews and this guy is like, whatever. Okay, I'm not prepared to do any interviews. Prior to that, I had given everyone a book called *"The Secret Relationship between Blacks and Jews"* written by the historical research department of the Nation of Islam given to me by Brother James Bomb, (James Allen) which was given to him by Don Muhammad in Boston. I duplicated it, gave it out to everyone. I had read it several times before I even got to D.C. to do that particular interview with David Mills.   So, sitting down and talking to David Mills, I had already had *"The Secret Relationship between Blacks and Jews"* on my mind, the tension in the group, Chuck blowing me off..."you do the interview," I'm sitting there with Andreas and we are talking to David Mills and we are talking about the music industry, who controls

11

the music industry, laying out names, and dates and books and all kinds of information. So, I said "I dealt with this question before with a group of journalists in England. If I had been talking about this for months and months and months for the whole European tour and I get back to America and it is nothing different. It is common knowledge with myself and Andreas, common knowledge with the people in our group, definitely common knowledge with Hank, Chuck, about the Jewish question. I even had the discussion with Bill Adler and some of the other Jewish people at Def Jam and at Rush and at Rhythm Method. Ron Scholer and Ed Chalpin and some other people so this wasn't like a surprise; this is being talked about all the time so the quotes that I think that were misquoted were *"...the Jews are responsible for the majority of wickedness [that went on around the globe]"* I can remember not saying. That is what I was quoted as saying, which to even look into that particular statement not only is it not correct, because to say the Jews are responsible for the majority of wickedness that went on around the globe I would have to know about the majority of wickedness that went on around the globe, which is impossible...I'm not the best knower Allah is. Then, not only knowing that, I would have to know who is at the crux of all of the problems in the world and then blame Jewish people, which is not correct.

SR: So all of this took place in that initial interview in Europe, in London?

PG: Those specific statements? No, in DC.

SR: But where they came from, or where David Mills heard them, was that at that initial interview?

PG: Right, exactly. I think he was repeating in his own words what he thought these other writers were saying that I said, and that is not true. I've had debates with Lyor Cohen for hours and days when I was on tour. None of this stuff came out like this, twisted, distorted. I was repeating the same thing over and over, so I don't see how anyone could have got it twisted. Jewish people exercise a certain amount of control in Law, in Education, in the music industry, politics, the media, and in Hollywood and this is known. You don't have to question Griff about that, hell; you can go on the internet and find that. Back then, you had to go to microfiche in the Library and look up who controlled or owned what. Read "The Media Monopoly," by Ben H. Bagdikian, but since it was condensed in a book called "The Secret Relationship between Blacks and Jews" the work was already done. I had the names, places, people, companies largely controlled by Jewish people. Watch and study the movie "Empire of their Own" by Neal Gabler. Then the question of the slave trade came up and that was already documented also. So, I knew who owned slaves, and how many slaves they owned, and the slave ships that they owned, the names of the ships, the 'good ship Jesus', the "holy mary" and the "grace of god" and the insurance companies that were started by them, how they insured the ships and the slaves. The conversation went from music to who owned slaves in present day and the past in Jewish history. What is the difference between a Zionist and a Jew? All of that was coming up. By the time I read back from what I supposedly had said in the Village Voice a week or so later...I was like "Wow, I didn't even say that." But by then it was too late because you had every Jewish person now taking pot shots and every ignorant Negro at the time was like "Man, why did he say that? Man, you're ruining Public Enemy. He's doing this....." So now, I became the enemy of the enemy inside of public enemy.

SR: **So were you expressing your own view or opinion, or where you expressing the sentiment of the whole group?**

PG: That's a very touchy question because even in the context of what the individuals in the group believe, they had the same information I had. Now, whether or not they were in that position as the Minister of Information or the spokesperson to do an interview then they were probably not, I was. Now, were they Griff's beliefs I sure thought it was because we were personal friends of Minister Farrakhan; we were as close to the Nation of Islam as hair to a rabbit's ass, so yes, I'm thinking that. Anybody would think that because it wasn't me who said "Farrakhan is a prophet and I think you ought to listen to," "a follower of Farrakhan don't tell me that you understand 'til you hear the man." That wasn't Griff's statement, those weren't Griff's words and more statements that we were talking about our relationship with the Nation of Islam and the philosophy and the ideology. You know we sampled Malcolm, Khalid, Ava Muhammad, Minister Farrakhan and other brothers and sisters from black radical organizations. All of which made up our rhetoric on and off stage throughout Public Enemy's early history. The Nation of Islam's history from way back since Master Fard Muhammad, Elijah Muhammad, right on through, we were sampling stuff, whatever. So, I'm thinking hell yeah! This is what we believe, this is what we think, this is how we feel. Come to find that the majority of people involved with PE were pig eating Christians.

SR: **So, what is now your philosophy, or perspective on Jewish and Black relations? Has it changed since that time?**

PG: My view or relationship?

SR: **Your view of the relationship.**

PG: Yes, of course, simply because I know and understand Jewish pain and Jewish hurt by meeting with Jewish people and going to the Holocaust museums on two different continents. I think I am more sensitive to Jewish pain and Jewish struggle as I am about Black people. I think in reading what took place between the relationship between Blacks and Jews since then to now, I see how Jewish people can take something like that and say "Look, we don't want to hear anything derogatory in reference to us." Are you following me? I can see how that would be very sensitive to Jewish people and they would come after Public Enemy. I can see that. But, what I don't understand is when our pain and suffering is put on the table no one seems to feel anything, no one seems to care, even what's going on now, I can roll you back to a recent history and we can roll ourselves back past the slave trade. You know, I can give you probably 20,000 years of history if we had the time and then we can look at the other people on the planet and say where are the other people at, no one came to our aid. Now, experimenting with Black women post slavery, where was the outcry? What went down in Rwanda, where was the outcry? What is going down in Darfur, where is the outcry? We can talk about political prisoners that are languishing in prison right now, where is the outcry? I can go from Tuskegee Syphilis experiments to chemical biological warfare by the United States government and other governments, where is the outcry? We can talk about AIDS alone, where is the outcry. We could talk about the millions of bones that are in the Atlantic Ocean, I can talk about reparations, where is the outcry? I could go on and on and on, and on, no one is that d_mn sensitive about Black people's plight. So, understanding Black people's plight and feeling it and understanding that, sh_t, I can understand how Jewish people feel. Hell, I wouldn't want anyone saying anything about Black people, but they do and get away with it. But, we don't have NBC, ABC, CBS and CNN to tell our story as much as they tell their story. We can't fire people. We can't rearrange rock groups and organize the media to destroy people's character. We can't order assassinations like these people do through the Mossad and the CIA and even blackwater. We can't lynch people in the media, crucify people, we can't do that, because we don't own the networks, they do.

SR: So do you believe you were crucified in the media?

PG: Hell yeah! Like a Black Jesus. Crucified. A lot of people want to stake that claim, but hell no, I was the one pierced in the side, blood dripping, hands nailed because now I can't work for myself because the group kicked me out. I can't use these hand to carve out a living and earn money for my family and feed my babies because they posted my picture in the paper and on the news as a hater of Jews. They worked to isolate me and force Chuck to kick me out of the group. The individuals; Chuck, Hank, Bill Stephanie, James, Roger and some other people, Mike and Flav got together and just said he don't need to be here. So my hands were nailed. A crown of thorns put on my head, now they are squeezing my brains until I can't even think. So all of the revolutionary thoughts that would come from a revolutionary are now dripping from my skull down the side of my face. Hung up next to two thieves. Spit on, mocked, lied on, talked about. Feet were nailed; can't travel because everywhere I go, I've got to deal with this. Jewish people dogging my trail. So, hell yeah, I was crucified if you want to look at it like that. I had to carry my own cross, which was heavy as hell. Christians don't talk to me about Jesus I lived it.

SR: Did David Mills actually call you an anti-Semite in his article. Did he actually use the wording that you were an anti-Semite, or that you made anti-Semitic references?

PG: No, never said it. He said that he could see how Jewish people could take this as you being anti-Semite. That is what he said. Now mind you now, shortly after we got started, his white Jewish girlfriend walked in and sat next to him. So, now the complexion of the conversation changed. It was no longer brothers sitting here talking, and several times I told him to turn the tape recorder off. Now, how he came up with some of the statements he came up with, wow, I don't know because at different intervals, I was asking him to turn the tape recorder off.

SR: Okay, well, in a follow up article in The Washington Times by David Mills, he states here that what you said at the 930 Club, in an interview, was that "the Jews are wicked." That "God promised the Jews a land they could call their own, why did they have to take it from the Palestinians?" Do you recall making that statement?

16

PG: Yes. I made that particular statement. Yes. Now, when you say when I said," the Jews are wicked," that was coming off a statement prior to that. So, then if I had to be grammatically correct, those Jews that I am talking about this particular situation are wicked, but it doesn't read that way. Chuck and other people said they were not Jews but Zionist and answered them by saying, *"Zionist Jews."* I was at the 930 Club and I was talking about a ring that I use to wear, it was a star and crescent. It was studded with diamonds. It was a ring given to me by Terminator X. And when we were talking about the diamond trade and we talking about the DeBeers, and I was starting to mention the families who controlled the diamonds. *Cecil Rhodes and the scholarships* and that kind of thing. That is what I was talking about. So, I said the Jews are wicked, those particular Jews that I am talking about, yes, that which they were doing was and is wicked. How did it end up with me saying that Jews were wicked?

SR: You were misquoted.

PG: Yes, exactly.

SR: So were your statements simply taken out of context?

PG: Do I believe right now that those particular Jews that I was talking about that run and own the diamond trade are wicked? Hell yeah! Hell yeah, they are wicked.

SR: So, if you can expound a little more on the context of what you were conveying to David Mills at this 930 Club.

PG: I wasn't talking to him. I was doing an interview with someone else. In fact, 2 or 3 of us during the interview and the question came up because whoever was interviewing me then had also read the stuff from Europe. So, he said *"Okay, you are doing quite well. You claim that Jewish people control the diamond trade in South Africa and your*

17

people are suffering. I see you are doing quite well you have a ring on with diamonds in it." (Laughter) So, when he made that statement, I said "Yeah this ring that was given to me by Terminator X. It is the Star and Crescent." I started to break it down and we started to go into the diamond trade and who controls it.

SR: So, was there ever a direct conversation interview with David Mills under the scope of this is an interview and you are being recorded?

PG: No, that interview that happened at the Holiday Inn was set up for Chuck. I sat in for Chuck to do the interview. We started talking about music. And it was one of those by the way; you did interviews saying that, I'm just curious; do you really believe Jewish people control the music industry. Well here is the proof. It is not coming from me here is the proof and I had the books with me and I laid them out.

SR: What do you believe was the reason then for David Mills misconstruing your words?   Do you think it was on purpose or just a misunderstanding of what you were saying?

PG: Role forward. Look at him now. We've done research of where he is now? In Hollywood, big time writer. You see he got rewarded for that traitorous act. Let's look at Clinton, he was the same one pulled that same trick, that same snitching ass sh_t with Sista Souljah who, when Sista Souljah said, in quoting *Bobby E. Wright, she said to Clinton that black people, we don't kill whites because we haven't been trained to kill whites"* and this is something Bobby E. Wright said. That is of our cultural experience. We haven't been trained to kill whites; we have been trained to kill one another. David Mills claim of fame is interviewing Sista Souljah and that he recorded an interview with Professor Griff, Souljah's 'kill whitey' comment and Griff's 'anti-semetic' comments. Not only that they rewarded him with a big time position, he is a big Hollywood writer now. He had his white girlfriend, you know, I think it was deliberate. I think he was sent out to do that particular interview with me because he had already known about Professor Griff. It was no secret on the Jewish question. Because most thought I took the side of the Palestinian.....no no no I take the side of truth.

SR: After the articles began to come out and the media frenzy began some say that you had "gotten off message" of the group Public Enemy. Had you gotten off the message of Public Enemy?

PG: Yes.

SR: How so?

PG: If I am rolling with my crew, I shouldn't be talking to the cats on the corner right now, and we have been together since knee high to a frog and we have done all kinds of crazy stuff as we do in the Hood with one another doing whatever we do with one another, and because I am the Minister of Information and I am gathering all this information and I am doing the interviews, if you felt that I was saying something that wasn't in sync with what the group was about then you should have pulled my coat and said "Yo, that is not cool man. We don't even need to do that. The strategy is let's do this, how we are going to approach that, this is how we are going to do." Pull my coat, and then we roll because we have done this for everything else. Do you understand what I am saying? I am talking to the average cat out there now. You and your man are trying to bag some chicks, don't you come up with a strategy on how you are going to go about it? You understand what I am saying? You may send your man over there as a front man to get the numbers and the digits and then you hook up a little bit later on after the party and hook up at the Waffle House or whatever, but none the less, it is still a strategy. So how come someone didn't say, "Yo, we are not talking about devils and demons and wicked people, and white people and whatever, whatever, we are sticking to trying to raise up our people, and we need to stick to that message. Let's stick to what Malcolm said, let's stick to what Dr. King said. Let's follow the Black Panthers way of doing things. Let's start a feed the homeless, or breakfast program." Ok, so like, no one said anything. Remember, we were only supposed to be in this thing for 2 years. Get in, shock them, get out. Are you following me? So, if I was going off course, someone should have said "Yo, you chill with that. Wo, this is what we are about. Let's stick to that."

SR: Okay.

PG: No one said that at all.

SR: So, had it been somebody else doing the interview...Had Chuck, or Flava actually made it to do the interview, would they have said something similar if that same question was posed to them?

PG: Yes, of course. They would have said something similar, or bite their tongue and not tell the truth and not speak truth to power. Yet, you can go all over the globe with all these tours and make all these songs in reference to pointing out who the enemy is, but when it comes to the Jewish question you don't want to say anything about Jewish involvement in the slave trade or the diamond trade or whatever. You're being a hypocrite. You are being a traitor.

SR: Some fans mentioned that what they wanted to know was what was the principle you were trying to uphold in the statements that you made even though those statements were obviously, as you said, misconstrued and misquoted. But, in the spirit of what you were presenting in those interviews that had taken place, what principle were you trying to uphold?

PG: The principle of self determination. All the principles that was given to us in Nguzu Saba, all the principles that was given to us, laid out by our brothers and sisters in ancient, classical civilization; all principles laid out not only by Nobel

Drew Ali, Marcus Garvey, Elijah Muhammad. All those principles that was laid out for Public Enemy was suppose to be about and keeping those principles intact and using those principles to raise the conscious level of our people. That was what I was trying to do, but, we had to remove the buffer. We had to talk about our open enemy as all of our leaders who came before us had to do. I am no different from them. Did not Marcus Garvey have to deal with his enemy and traitors within? So did I. Did Elijah Muhammad have to deal with hypocrites? Didn't Elijah Muhammad have to deal with white people sending in black people in to sabotage, to be agent provocateurs? Yes, of course. Did we not go over the history of the CO-INTEL PRO? J. Edgar Hoover's CO-INTEL PRO counter intelligence program? Did not the Mau-Mau have the same experiences? Did not the ANC...African nation congress have to kill there traitors. I could mention black organizations from now on. Did they have to deal with white people and Negroes alike? Yes! So the principle was to point out and find out what we were doing, this is our plan, we know we are going to have some opposition as Chuck D. said early on, we probably won't be living to see this? We will probably be dead or in jail. We pointed out the enemy itself. This is why we went into the prisons, this why we did free concerts, this is why we gave away free tickets, free CD's, this is why we went in the Hood, this is why we have Cyphers on the corner, this is why we met black people wherever they were. Are you following me? Instill that principle of self determination and do something for self.

SR: So after the article and the interviews, was the reaction different overseas in Europe than it was in the United States?

PG: The reaction was different 2 or 3 days later. When I first told Chuck and other people you know some of the stuff I laid out it was hunched shoulders and not like you never said this sh_t before. All became a different story when it hit the Village Voice. So now they start to change their minds.

21

Now, Jewish people are galvanizing their energy and their efforts. Relationships are being questioned. Snipers are sitting on top of roofs now taking pot shots at Def Jam thinking that Professor Griff is sitting in the offices. Oh, people are coming after us now. People are dogging our trail. People are being put among us, that kind of thing, people are backing away from me like I had Aids. So, I say to the people now take even the statements they said I said and put them under a microscope and see if it is true.

SR: So, if you could take us back you mentioned it very briefly, explain a little further, what was the group's initial response after the article and the interview?

PG: We had a show that night. So it was like, so what? Chuck even told the audience about the interview whatever, whatever, and that he (meaning me) doesn't bite his tongue, we speak truth to power, yada, yada, yada, ya. There are some people that are holding us back, yada, yada, yada, whoop de whoop de whoop, as he mentioned in "Welcome to the Terrordome"…"Crucifixion ain't no fiction, So called chosen frozen, Apology made to whoever pleases, Still they got me like Jesus, I rather sing, bring, think reminisce' Bout a brother while I'm in sync, Every brother ain't a brother cause a color, Just as well could be undercover. Backstabbed, grabbed a flag, from the back of the lab, told a Rab get off the rag." You know that kind of stuff. That stuff was nothing to us that was common knowledge.

SR: Well then, obviously, the sentiment of the group changed. When did the tone change?

PG: It had to do with private conversations among them and as I mentioned to you, I was mad as hell. I had told Minister Farrakhan, I said, "Man they were marked for death." I said this sitting at his dining room table. I said, "look I've got

22

pictures of all these niggas! They are dead." That is when the Minister told me to leave them alone.

SR: And who were you talking about?

PG: Public Enemy. All of them. James, Roger, Mike, Chuck, Hank, Bill, Harry, Little James. I excused Keith Shockley, Terminator X, Eric Saddler, they were cool with me. You understand what I am saying? A lot of people from where we lived in and around us thought it was betrayal, that Chuck was being a traitor. The average cat in the street was like "Huh? Over some crackers? Man f_ck them crackers." Man, they were like, forget that! You don't disassociate yourself from your homies because some white boy said you said something about some crackers...man f_ck all of them. That's the average sentiment of the brothers in the street. So, Dr. Alim Muhammad, Leonard Muhammad who is related to Minister Farrakhan, Hank Shockley, Chuck D, these niggas was at the top of my list. I'm telling you, I'm gunning for them. How can you say...? One minute we cool, and this is common knowledge, next minute it hits the press, the Village Voice, and now, all of a sudden, I'm a stage prop? Now, I'm not really part of the group and I'm this that and the other. Some f_cking cowards. That was my sentiment at the time you understand? And those same brothers that I had recruited as S1W's, they betrayed me also. Now, The 98 Posse and all of them was like, "Yeah, we'll do these niggas, f_ck'em." That was my crew, those were my people.

SR: Some reported that you were instructed to, I guess so called, get back on message of the group, yet you refused. Is that true?

PG: That's not true. Get back on message the way they was conveying it then was, go apologize. F_ck them, and f_ck the cracker! That was my attitude. Apologize for what? My father told me you never apologize for the truth.

SR: Okay. On February 4ᵗʰ, 1990 the L.A. Times...

PG: Wait, that's like telling Jesus to go back and apologize and take all the prophetic things he said back. Like John 8:44...That's crazy!

SR: What I was going to mention was a February 4ᵗʰ 1990 L.A Times article by Steve Hochman where he states that " He," (meaning you), "is eager now to say his widely quoted remarks was the result of ignorance and that means he (meaning you) regrets that he made them." Was this an accurate reporting?

PG: No. Definitely not. That mess. I remember that particular talk with that gentleman and two others.   They say, Ignorance is simply truth ignored. Ignored, not only is it factual documents.   There are segments of Jewish people that don't agree with the Zionist plot established in the state of Israel.   Now, when I agree with those Jews, is one question I can honestly say I don't believe them.   If I go along with the Zionist plot, if God is going to promise you, if you are the Chosen people, and God's going to promise you a land you don't have to steal it. You're like a bush kid, like we said back in the day, you don't have to take nobody's property. You really don't. If it is promised to you then wait on the promise. Wait on God to deliver the promise. God says in the scripture God changes not. So God will keep his promise. You understand what I am saying? Regret that I admit for those particular statements if the statements were quoted the way I said them, then everything would be fine. But, if you misquote them to get sensational news headlines, then hell no, I can't figure how to leave those particular statements alone.

SR: So, when Mr. Hochman mentioned ignorance as we just talked about was he talking about your own ignorance or was he talking about the way he presented the article?

PG: Yes, yes.

SR: Your own ignorance or the ignorance of those who misunderstood you?

PG: No, he is talking about my ignorance and he is absolutely correct because I wasn't taking into account Jewish sentiment, Jewish sensitivity.   Sh_t, the average black person, especially then at the age I was at then coming up out of Roosevelt Long Island, we didn't have any relationship with Jewish people.   They were the f_cking landlords and we rented.   They were the store owners.   They owned everything.   We didn't have a relationship with Jewish people.   Now, if somebody out there can prove this wrong, please call me.   We did not have a relationship with Jewish people.   Not as a collective, as individuals we did. But hell, I'm growing up on Roosevelt Island, 7th child of 13. The 12th child actually, but the 7th son.   I ain't had no relationship with Jewish people.   So to know how Jewish people felt over the entire history of Jewish people, to know what Jewish people went through...Man I didn't know nothing else, so it is my ignorance.

SR: Why didn't the group, specifically Chuck D back you up?

PG: In the beginning, he did.   Even after the sh_t storm, even after that he did.   But he was being wishy-washy.   He backed me up about 4 or 5 times.   I mean, we locked ourselves in a hotel room in Chicago and literally, physically cried that this sh_t was going on.   You understand what I am saying?   He's always wanting to back me up, but he was getting hit from 3 different angles.   And he had to sacrifice Griff or keep the group going.   My sentiment and the people around me was like the sh_t was suppose to crash in two years anyway, just about that time.   In '86, '87, '88, the sh_t happened in '89 it was a rap.

SR: Well, after the supposed comment that you made, some journalists thought you were expendable.

PG: Hold on just a minute, let me add on here. It was Chuck D's group from the beginning. What was Bill Stephanie, Ed Shockley, Harry Allen, all of the S1W's was paying lip service, and if any one of them wanted to debate me, they could have. No one said anything, just for me to apologize and take it back. David Mills came back and apologized. But you don't read that. Came back and apologized and we had an open forum, put on by the Nation of Islam at Howard University and they brought me in through the back door and David Mills was there and he apologized. He came to Hempstead, 510 South Franklin, at our studio, upstairs and he sat with them and he told them, "Yeah, I did my research, Griff was right. Not only were they involved in the slave trade, and the diamond trade, cotton and all kinds of minerals, precious minerals taken out of the soil of Africa and brought to America." But you don't read that. Two people apologized, but you don't read that.

SR: Did he actually publish his apology?

PG: Nope. Not at all.

SR: So he did it in some public arena but not officially in writing?

PG: Exactly.

SR: Okay well, the question we were going to ask before...

PG: Wait, wait, wait I'm sorry to keep cutting you off...

SR: No, its okay, come on

PG: But the stuff keeps coming back to me it's like isn't it ironic we can't even find the interview?

SR: Yes.

PG: To this day now, we can't find the interview. Nowhere. Isn't it ironic all that stuff burned up in my house fire and none of this stuff is available now? Someone has it somewhere and we put it out on the internet for anyone that has it can e-mail it to us or where they can find it.

SR: So the original article and interviews you did have copies of that?

PG: And the actual Village Voice and the actual transcripts.

SR: And those were burned in the house fire last year.

PG: Gone, Right.

SR: Well, continuing with the questions, after the comments you were supposed to have made, there were some journalists who thought you were expendable because you were simply as quoted by Diana Maychick, a stage prop or a dancer for Public Enemy. What do you think of them?

PG: F_ck'em, and stage props don't end up on CNN. Stage props don't get interviewed for 20 years, stage props don't get mentioned in every single article in every single news source. Stage props aren't still warrant boxes and boxes of dialogues dealing with Black and Jewish issues. Stage props don't get that much play. Stage props don't get television time and air time on the radio. Stage props don't get that. If I am expendable, and I'm a stage prop and a dancer, when was the last time they interviewed the dancers from Heavy D and the Boys? When was the last time they interviewed Eddie Hamlin's dancers as well as they....When was the last time they interviewed the dancers on Soul Train. When was the last time any of those dancers were on CNN and the nightly news and the Daily news, and the New York Times, the New York Post? Stop, stop that.

SR: Do you think the group, specifically Chuck D. handled the situation as best as they could at the time and I'm referring

27

to of course, many statements that Chuck made apologizing for what you said and separating the group from you? A quote from one of those letters was "Professor Griff's timing and choice of words or attitude reflected in his statement is not representative of the program of Public Enemy or reflective of the Minister of Information for the group?" So, do you think that Chuck and the group handled the situation as best they could at that particular time?

PG: Absolutely not. Chuck D. had a press conference without me, signed a sworn statement against me and when you hear stuff like that that don't even sound like something Chuck wrote. Black people don't talk like that. Am I right or wrong? Some f_cking chick in the office somewhere typed that up at the behest of Bill Adler or somebody, or Russell Hustle Simmons and Chuck signed on to that madness. Please, how are you going to sign something like that and turn around and face black people? The same black people we are helping them to redeem their life? Coming out of prison, you understand what I am saying? The projects...please and timing? When was I supposed to say this? I've been saying it. You understand my choice of words. What other words? This is their language. This is the language they forced down our throats. This is their b_stard language called English. Should I have used the King's English and said it more pleasant? Please, no, we are from the f_cking Hood, do you understand what I am saying? Stop.

SR: Okay, why do you believe they allowed you to be the sacrificial lamb?

PG: Thinking that I would dry up and blow away. That the group could push on. Long as these nigga's can still buck dance on stage, tap dancing and eat watermelon. That the group would push forward. As long as it is an entertainment part of Public Enemy where they can do shows and they have enough songs in the catalog and up to that point it will carry them through. Yeah, we don't need him. Sh_t, we have done shows without Flava, done shows without Chuck in the early days, so, getting rid of me was nothing to them. They kind of figured I didn't contribute anything, just a couple of miniscule kind of vocals every now and then on a song. Unless you piecing those songs apart, you don't know that's me, unless somebody tell you, you understand what I am saying? The producers, Def Jam, Sony, Bill Adler, Bill Stephanie, Hank Shockley, those guys in and around Chuck, they was like, "Well you don't really need him, you can do X, Y and Z. But now, how you going to face that hardcore dude in the street now? You're not going to be able to do that. So, I was told to leave them alone and I followed Minister Farrakhan's order and I did. I didn't make no dis records, I didn't sabotage anything. I left the offices alone, none of them got harmed, they were able to live their lives.

SR: You talked about it a little bit, but what were your true feelings as you began to see your comrades were not going to stand in solidarity with you?

PG: F_cking traitors man. You know, if this was a true military, if this was a true nation of people, the Mau-Mau use to put inner tubes around their traitors and douse them with gasoline and set their _ss on fire. Some organizations and military units use to tie the feet together and tie a rope around them, drag them through the street while they are on fire and people beat them with sticks for selling out your people. Then they use to hang them upside down, tar and feather them and beat them to death. Some traitors use to get stoned to death. Some traitors got their eyes, hands and tongue cut out. Are you following me? I thought of all of that and then some. For these people going back on their word. In the Holy Qu'ran, it teaches how Allah prepares a lake of fire for the hypocrite. Hell yeah, I was ready to do them, if it were not, I swear, if it was not for Minister Farrakhan's voice ringing in my ear, those niggas would be dead. Dead. Dead. Then I would dig the mothaf_ckers up and kill them again. I have no room in my heart for a traitor. None.

SR: Had the group supported you do you think Public Enemy would have had the impact they eventually came to have?

PG: Probably more so, because the level of respect that we would have had, just from the average person in the street, man, like wow, you know something, you'll went through that and stuck together, I really admire that. Just like you would say some of your relatives were breaking up, getting a divorce, that ugly thing. They worked it out and stayed together for the children's sake, for the family's sake. Yeah, it's always embraced by the people, not only here on this continent, but throughout the globe. There are revolutionaries today as we see America's fake war on terrorism, you understand what I am saying? We the human family must stick together and if these people are b_stards in the house, trouble makers in the house then we have to put them in the time out corner. But for these people to uproot Public Enemy, and the age old trick of divide and conquer and you see it happening. You say no, that's divide and conquer, don't let that happen. That's the enemy in us doing that. It's like nothing those brothers were hearing at that time, even though privately, some of them were coming to me like, "Yo, that's f_cked up."

SR: That leads to my next question. There were some who sided with you. Did anyone else support you?

PG: Yes, Ghetto Boys, Ice T, I can remember Ice T, I can remember Lynch Mob, I can remember talking to the average guy in the street, Just Ice. I can remember talking to hip hop heads in the hood, personal conversations, I could go on and on, but there was just the average rap head was like, "Yo, I don't understand that sh_t, for real man." Red Alert, Chuck Chill Out. I can remember some Jewish people just in personal and private conversations just like "I'm sure you didn't say that?" Cause they knew me and I think Ice T was one of those dudes that really, really stuck by me. Willie D and Bushwick Bill taking a bold stand, and they weren't backing down man, not at all. Some cats, Lynch Mob, I remember having a conversation with Ice Cube and Wren I talked to Tupac and Trech from Naughty by Nature, "Man we don't give a f_ck about crackers like that."

SR: What about within the group, in the label, like the immediate...

PG: Like I said, Chuck on and off. Big ups to Eric Saddler, Keith Shockley, these cats were not going for this sh_t. Huh? The hell with a cracker. (*This was the white man on the plantation with the title cracker because he cracked the whip when they wanted a slave beat*) That was the attitude. We didn't have a relationship with Jewish people like that, because hell, half the time you didn't know the person you were dealing with was Jewish, they hide their real true identity so we didn't have a relationship like that.

SR: Were you dismissed or fired from the group?

PG: Both. Two or three different times. Then Chuck said some homo _ss sh_t like Griff is going through counseling to deal with his problem.

SR: So this followed immediately following the controversy or sometime there after?

PG: No. They were throwing me up on their shoulders. Hooray, hooray. You bringing truth to power, then when the sh_t hit the Village Voice, that is when Alim Muhammad and Leonard Farrakhan Muhammad from the Nation of Islam, f_cking cowards. (Laughter) They got in Chuck's head, after that, my _ss was gone. I was gone. F_cking hypocrite's man, after that sh_t, I was gone; they through my _ss under the bus.

SR: So you of course, have had lifelong relationships with comrades in the group...

31

PG: Wait, I use to live with Hank Shockley's family, me and his family was tight, I couldn't get any tighter. I use to live with them. Me and Chuck grew up since we were young.

SR: So, how were these relationships affected during the controversy?

PG: Me and Dorothy Boxley, Hank's mom, we remained close. She didn't believe that madness. Me and Judy Ridenhour, Chuck's mom, we're tight; Mr. "R," to this day, it's all love. But they sat me down..."Now Griff, you know..." one of those conversations if you know what I mean. "You know what kind of positions you put my son in," and I understand.

SR: Now you talked about how you felt with or behind your comrades, your brothers in this group not standing with you, but the actual separation from the group, how did you feel about being fired from the group?

PG: How personal can I get? This is like you go in for an operation and your homeboy is dying and he needs a lung, and it's like I got two, you can get one. It's really, really personal because it wasn't about me, it wasn't about Chuck, it wasn't about the Bomb Squad, it wasn't about Flava, it was about Black people and that was all I cared about. I didn't give a f_ck about music, if we were doing double Dutch, I was fine, I could speak through that, whatever it was, I cared about Black people and just like a lot of people are having a hard time dealing with Minister Farrakhan behind the Malcolm thing, that's how it was with me and Chuck. D_mn. So, I went through the Malcolm, Elijah thing, Farrakhan, Malcolm thing, ok so now it was the Chuck, Griff thing, and all of this is very painful. Hell, I lived through the Khalid, Farrakhan thing, now I'm living through the Ray Hagins, Ashra Kwesi thing. It's critical.

SR: So, the reports that said your attitude towards being separated from the group was, "I'm going to do my own solo project anyway"?

PG: That's a lie. That's an absolute f_cking lie. I wasn't an artist. I wasn't a recording artist, I was the Minister of Information. Guess who got me my deal? Chuck D. Chuck D. got me my recording contract with Luke at Luke Skywalker records in Miami. I wasn't thinking about making any album. Go back and listen to my first album, I was doing poetry. The Last Asiatic Disciples were rapping, so that is an absolute lie. I don't have any rapping skills, I still don't. Being truthful, I wasn't a rapper. I didn't give a f_ck about that, no.

SR: Well, tell us, what happened to you personally, immediately following this controversy and being separated from the group? Were there threats on your person, your well-being was that put into jeopardy?

PG: Well, got threatened, children got threatened, relationships were being torn apart, didn't know who I could trust. Ended up getting poisoned in New Orleans, went back to Miami. It got worse when I ended up in the hospital, flew to Wimbledon, England with some of the Last Asiatic Disciples and with my wife, Kristie Eugene at the time. She bounced, left me there, bed ridden, pneumonia didn't have the use of my legs from the waist down, laying up in the bed, in white-_ss England. Having to be cared for by some white women (Laughter), some related to one the Rastas and or the promoters who got us there. That sh_t was ugly. That sh_t was really, really ugly. Just to come back to North Miami Beach to find the divorce papers in the mail, or the threatening phone calls still. My wife talking about she was tired of sleeping with the gun under the pillow, people threatening us in the middle of the night, notes on the car and all that kind of sh_t. Yeah.

SR: As you talk about that, you were called in many different articles Swine, hate monger, bigot amongst so many other derogatory names, obviously this affected you...to what extent?

PG: I think it affected me to the point that I was afraid for the people around me. Sh_t, I did not give a f_ck, I really didn't care. I was afraid for the people around me and at that time, kind of thinking Minister Farrakhan tied my hands, I can't kill these niggas, I can't really defend myself. It's like, wife bounced, I'm there in North Miami Beach among Jewish people by my d_mn self, working at Luke records who didn't give a f_ck about me. Half of his staff was Jewish and my songs came out on his label, I was f_cked. They were sabotaging that sh_t like... So, what do you do?

SR: As the controversy continued to snowball, how did the group, Third Base factor into all of this? There was some drama that came up around this.

PG: I think they did something that was very untimely, and the thing that hurt my heart was not that they disrespected Malcolm and this buffoonery imitating black people stuff. Doing stuff in front of the Audubon ballroom where Malcolm X was assassinated. The thing that hurt my heart was that Chuck was there. Chuck was there and didn't say anything. So, like man, you are straight up p_ssy. You let these two little f_cking white _ss Jewish dudes disrespect Black people, disrespect Malcolm. F_ck that, let's role on them man. "No man, they were only making fun." We can't make fun of them and the Holocaust, why would you allow that? So, I picked up a f_cking typewriter and was going to hit the b_stard up side his head. So they called the police on me, and I was about to be thrown out of Def Jam's office. F_ck, S1W's sitting around; nobody doing nothing. So the white boys can dis me, dis Malcolm. Everybody that believed in Malcolm and felt so strong about Malcolm, wearing X hats and buttons, but when two white boys disrespect Malcolm, no one wants to do anything? F_ck that. My crew was out gunning for those crackers. Seriously!

SR: So reportedly that led to the final separation from the group Public Enemy is that right?

PG: Right, because if you go back and look at the album cover, I was there that day in Def Jam, we went ahead and shot the photo shoot. So, I'm there on Fear of A Black Planet, but that is the day they got rid of my _ss, they called the police on me.

SR: In summation, what do you want people to know about the entire anti-Semitic situation?

PG: My statements in reference to the Jewish question were not intended to destroy or hurt anyone as individuals, or collectively the Jewish people's history in knowing the plight of the Jewish people. You know, what they went through, we can times that by one hundred to tell the Black people's plight from Africa to America and even before then and even after that. So I sympathize, and even empathize with what Jewish people went through. And if it came off really mean spirited and ugly, I already apologized for that. The spirit in which I delivered it. That kind of sensitive information, trying to reach people, you don't give it in that kind of spirit. That I apologized for several times and those individual Jews I was friends with I went to apologize to them personally, because I didn't want them to take it personal. Did I have to grow from there, from that point, yeah, because when I was a child I spoke as a child. But that sentiment was what you felt today in this particular interview. Rolling my mind back, I am more mature today. If I was asked those same questions today I would probably answer them in a more sophisticated way because I'm more mature. How we deal with traitors, we still have not figured out a way. How we deal with those that betray us, we still haven't figured out a way, but I really want Black people to know that we have a rich legacy, we have to study our history and those people responsible for the condition we are in, we still have to call it like we see it, plain and simple and we can't excuse them and no other people, including the black Africans on the African continent that helped us get into this situation, we cannot excuse them. All of them are going to be brought to the table of accountability and we are going to get reparations and we are going to deal with this question of Black people and reparations, and black people being free in a land that we can call our own. Now whether Jewish people want to apologize for what they've done, we are open to that. We are open to paying Black people back in the form of reparations, repairing the damage they have done. We don't have to call out the damage they have done. We are not going to call it out, but we are not going to let that question go, because I'm 49 years old now and a little bit more mature, I'm not letting that question go, not at all. We're going to answer those questions, now whether or not they want to have a relationship with us, that's on them.

SR: What do you want people to know about you?

PG: That I am my father's son. I'm more mature. I am a grandfather myself. I don't have any personal hatred against Jewish people or white people. I have a position I am going to stand on. Anyone would stand on their position. The Jew-ish question is a linguistic question, it is a religious question, it is a political question, it is a spiritual question, it is a nationalistic question, it is a philosophical question, it is a historical question, and of all of those if you come against me to debate me we are going to deal with all of those. Plain and simple, I am not going to back down off of it. I am not going to back down and apologize for the truth. History is what it is. I didn't write it, I inherited it. I didn't write it, I have to deal with it as it is and we have to correct the wrongs. Every time I have conversations like this I think of the millions that were lost in the middle passage. I think of the millions of blind, death and dumb today. Understand what I am saying? I have to be the voice of the voiceless. I am the ancestors speaking to me from within me to you.

SR: So with that said, what is your mission or your purpose here on planet Earth?

PG: I still have to raise the consciousness of our people, that's my mission. I've got to see us in a land we call our own. Now, we can carve out our own destiny and determine our own destiny. That's my mission plain and simple and I cannot let the legacy of Steve Biko, the Mau-Maus, Nat Turner, Harriet Tubman, I could go on and on, but I can't let that die not as long as my heart is beating, I cannot let that die, seriously. And all those brothers that came with the ultimate plan that I know is correct like the blueprint Elijah Muhammad, Amos Wilson, Dr. Frances Cress-Welsing all of our people laid out for us I know was 100 percent right and correct. I have to be able to implement that in a life curriculum. That is my mission.

SR: Have you since mended ways with the group?

PG: We are working on that. There are some brothers in there that hate my guts and I don't think that will change no time soon. It's just about the hatred that is there.

SR: What about you and Chuck?

PG: Oh, me and Chuck is fine. Me and Chuck are absolutely fine. We are men, we came together, we talked. Now don't get me wrong there are still some things that I don't agree with, but none the less, we can still love one another as brothers.

SR: Good. So are you currently an active member of Public Enemy?

PG: Currently, I am an active member in Public Enemy and have pulled back on the interviews and that kind of stuff because I am well able to speak for myself and those of us that share my sentiment, that's like minded, I can speak to them.

SR: Okay, all right, well is there anything else you would like to say before we close out?

PG: Just a few quotes; I am because we are, and revolution is not an event, it's a process, and one last thing I believe Frederick Douglass said, "We may not get all we pay for in life, but we sure pay for everything we get." That is it.

SR: Well, this is Sista Rah, also known as Rabiyah Karim-Kincey and Professor Griff of Public Enemy and we have been setting the record straight.

****

1998 Lethal Records/ Blackheart/ Mercury

ISH RUNS DOWNHILL
LA Weekly, 1989

Shortly before the June 1988 release of *It Takes a Nation of Millions to Hold Us Back*, Public Enemy did some alarming interviews in London. Quotable quotes like, "There's no place for gays." When God destroyed Sodom and Gomorrah, it was for that sort of behavior and If the Palestinians took up arms, went into Israel and killed all the Jews, it'd be alright so shocked the U.K. that to this day most Brit crits believe *Yo! Bum Rush the Show* is the great PE album. Odious as these sentiments are, though, the fact remains that there's no discernible homophobia or anti-Semitism (and only a touch of reverse racism) in the crew's recorded work. Furthermore, the offending bigmouth was neither Chuck D nor Flavor Flav, but PE's designated Minister of Information, Professor Griff, reputedly a Black Muslim, though one hears that Muslims don't trust Griff because he declines to observe Nation of Islam tenets while continuing to spout white-men-f_cked-dogs-in-the-Caucasus dogma. Soon word was that either Def Jam or PE itself had gagged Griff. When John Leland covered the group for the September 1988 *Spin*, he talked to Chuck D and only Chuck D, who first asserted, "I back Griff. Whatever he says, he can prove," then claimed, "People are gonna see that Griff said this, and in the same interview, I said something else." Obviously, Chuck was a little loose-lipped with Leland. But compared not just to Griff but to, oh, John Cougar Mellencamp, he was Noam Chomsky.

And there the matter lay. Long since platinum, *Nation of Millions* is now regarded as a milestone. Hank Shocklee is a remixer in full effect, Flavor Flav a street hero, Chuck D talking vanity label with MCA. And while no outsider would call their ideology consistent, gradually Public Enemy came to be seen as a politically promising public entity--at the very least, the chief reason second-generation B-boys adorn themselves with leather Africa medallions instead of dookie gold. Until May 22, when the Reverend Moon's ultraconservative D.C. daily *The Washington Times* published a one-on-one interview between Professor Griff and black reporter David Mills.

It's tempting to see this confrontation as a set-up, and in the usual journalistic sense it was, knowing Griff had a damaging story in him, Mills enticed him into giving it up. But after meeting Mills, an excitable young guy with a Southern drawl who could pass for Italian or Greek, I found it hard to see him as part of a rightwing conspiracy to rid the nation of up-and-coming Black Nationalist leaders (which is how many regard Al Sharpton's association with onetime D.A. candidate Vernon Mason, for instance). He's clearly appalled by both anti-Semitism and white racism; a month after his big moment he was arguing furiously with anyone who cocked an eyebrow at him that he had every right to research Jewish involvement in the slave trade. And in any case, Griff was aching to get sucker-punched. Forty minutes into their exchange, Mills kicked off the crucial segment of the interview by citing "an offhand remark" Griff had made on a TV interview a month before—"I think that's why they call it 'jewelry,' because the Jews in South Africa, they run that thing"--and Griff was off to the races.

This wasn't just anti-Zionism run amok; it was pure, paranoid, hate-filled anti-Semitism, with Henry Ford's notorious *The International Jew* a prime cited source. After making an exception for the "righteous" Jews "that are following the Torah given to them by Moses" (we'll meet these paragons again soon), Griff opined that "the majority of them [i.e., Jews]" are responsible for "the majority of the wickedness that goes on across the globe." He dared Jews to send "their faggot little hit men" after him, raved about how "the

Jews finance these experiments on AIDS with black people in South Africa," observed that "the Jews have their hands right around Bush's throat," and concluded that he must be speaking the truth because if he wasn't the Jew who owned CBS would long since have forced him, Griff, out of the group. In all these pronouncements, of course, the style of thought is as telling as the substance-- homophobic epithets, a lobby as a stranglehold, a single man 'owning' an enormous corporation. But faced with these rabid slanders, Chuck D declined to dissociate himself from his brother. As Mills recounted a later interview: "So as Chuck D sees it, true Jews aren't responsible for the world's wickedness. Maybe I would say people that *fronted* as Jews. I don't think they deserve the term Jew." Only paragons need apply.

Although Mills piece was reprinted May 29 in the Moonies' New York rag, the story lagged until RJ Smith picked it up in the *Village Voice* out June 14. (I should note that I get my paycheck from the *Voice* and count RJ a friend.) That was when the "sh_t storm" Chuck D predicted began. All kinds of gossip surfaced--the group's longsuffering label publicist Bill Adler (raised Jewish) had had enough, the group's up-and-coming private publicist Leyla Turkkan (raised Muslim) had had enough, Chuck was label-jumping, the group was breaking up. And the feces are still flying as I write, partly because instead of either sticking by Griff or disowning him, Chuck D tried to do both. To an extent this must have reflected genuinely divided loyalties--in the kindest construction, his personal ties pulled him one way and his own beliefs the other. There are even rumors that at one point in PE's inept damage control operation Chuck alone opposed ousting Griff from the group. At his most hysterical, he was dumb enough to phone Smith and hit him with some freestyle: "Listen to me, RJ, any sh_t that comes down on me, it's coming down on you. And that's a godd_mn threat! Write this down! I ain't gonna write no godd_mn white-boy liberal letter to the editor, no article either."

By June 19, with that gem already in Smith's next column, Chuck had chilled enough to sign a single-spaced two-and-a-half page statement ("TO ALL OFFENDED, CONCERNED AND

UNCONCERNED") announcing that Griff was no longer Public Enemy's Minister of Information. The wording was roundabout, never quite specifying whether Griff was dismissed for his stated ideas or his failings as a 'diplomat.' But the tone was thoughtful, informed, humane, and a little mad--in short, a rock critic's dream. Certainly no white admirer of the group could hope for an antiracist credo more explicit than "Black Power is only a self-defense movement that counterattacks the system of white world supremacy, not white people or the religious sects they choose." Next day, the statement was withdrawn. A new one, we were told, would be presented at a press conference the following morning.

The hot rumor was that Griff had been kicked out of PE altogether, and at around 11:15am in a modest conference room at Manhattan's Sheraton Centre that rumor came true, or so it seemed. Compared to a similar event almost exactly a decade earlier, when Elvis Costello tried to apologize for uttering the word 'nigger' in public, this one was small potatoes--a dozen or so print journalists, Mills included, and three TV crews who soon blew out the mike, thus almost silencing the star attraction, Chuck D and only Chuck D. It was also brief, with questions cut off after half an hour. Though at moments his wording could still be construed as more critical of Griff's timing than of his beliefs, Chuck D stated explicitly that 'the whole group' (which other members later denied) had dismissed Griff as a matter of 'discipline' for his failure to promulgate 'Public Enemy's program.' For once he came off truly righteous: "We are not anti-Jewish, we are not anti-anybody--we are pro-black, pro-black culture, pro-human race. Professor Griff's responsibility as Minister of Information for Public Enemy was to faithfully transmit those values--to everybody. In practice he sabotaged these values."

Chuck made clear that he still felt loyalty and admiration for PE's most diligent freelance scholar. But he also implied what many believed--that Griff's provocations had been deliberate, a way of getting back at the group for his diminished role. And at least three of Chuck's comments set him apart from black nationalist orthodoxy: he referred to Griff's 'offensive'--never 'anti-Semitic'--

43

comments as 'racism' ("You can't talk about attacking racism and be racist"), acknowledged that even blacks had participated in the slave trade ("though they got conquered too in the end"), and distinguished the Nation of Islam's economic program from the rest of its ideology ("I follow the Nation because Minister Farrakhan and the Nation show us economic self-sufficiency in America and that's my sole use for this information"). A lot of the time he seemed like the smartest guy at a dorm-room bull session. "I don't even want to get into the religion game," he told us, "because I just think religion throughout the years has been a conspiracy by the world leaders to trick the people." Right on.

There were predictable mutterings that Chuck had been forced to moderate his posture by CBS or MCA--people didn't say 'the Jews' only because they were in a state of raised consciousness. And clearly the pressure had been driving Chuck crazy--like all new stars and many old ones, he has a hellish time determining where private begins and public leaves off even under ordinary circumstances. It was my impression, however, that he wasn't bullsh_tting. Even better, it seemed conceivable that this grotesque incident would prove the catalyst that could inspire PE to top an album so epochal there was no reason to hope they'd ever get over it. But subsequent events haven't moved that way. The very next day, sources close to PE began reporting that the group had broken up, and soon it was official. "We're outta here," Chuck told an MTV interviewer. And sharing a bill with N.W.A at Philadelphia's Spectrum Sunday night--Griff didn't appear, although he was backstage--he announced that this would be Public Enemy's final performance. There was a small riot. Spectrum employees were assaulted. It was a mess.

For the moment, that's where the saga stands. It won't stop developing--Al Sharpton has been seen circling in PE's vicinity--and it's reasonable to hope that three or six or nine months down the road, after Spike Lee returns to the set and Chuck's label flops and Flavor Flav staggers under the weight of his own album, PE will regroup. But for the moment it's relatively stable, and we're stuck with a familiar rock and roll tragedy: well-meaning entertainers thrust into a prominence they can't handle. Even before the sh_t storm, Public Enemy was riden by the jealousies and thwarted egos that beset all newly successful groups, with special complications. At one point, Leyla Turkkan told Chuck that he wasn't equal to the leadership role she'd helped him achieve: "You're not learned enough, she pointed out. And while that's not the whole story (learning has never helped anybody cope with the brute exposure of fame), it's a contradiction endemic to an era when we expect political insight from rock heroes--think of Bono, Mellencamp, Prince. If the rock heroes are black nationalists, so much the worse-- although the sorry history of integration in this country has once again convinced many of us that some sort of black-power program is essential to the achievement of the most basic kind of black equality, the details of that program have escaped thinkers far more sapient than Chuck D. The best we can hope is that this latest setback will prove educational--the learn-from-our-mistakes/trials model. The worst we can fear is that it will serve to unloose the already overflowing backlog of desperation and paranoia on both sides of the color line.

E*DU*CA*RE
The Education of Professor Griff
When Richard Griffin, of Public Enemy fame, was interviewed on
May 9, 1989, he was quoted as saying, among other things,
that "Jews have a grip on America" and that they "have a
history of killing black men"

New Times by Greg Baker Published on July 11, 1990

O n May 9, 1989, Richard Griffin, better known as
Professor Griff, met with a writer from the Washington
Times for the purpose of an interview. The article resulting from
that tape-recorded session, published two weeks later, quoted Griff
as saying, among other things, that "Jews have a grip on America"
and that they "have a history of killing black men." Further, Griff
told writer David Mills that Jews are responsible for "the majority of
wickedness that goes on across the globe."

Sitting in a cramped, windowless office within the new Luke
Records complex in northeast Miami late last week, Professor Griff
recalls that fateful day ruefully. He still believes he was manipulated
by Mills. "It was supposed to be a musical interview," Griff says. "It
led into a discussion of Jewish control of the music industry, the
media, TV, and movies. It was music, music, music, and then he
slips in a question about who controls the music industry. I was
caught off guard, and it was at a time when there was a lot of tension
[among his musical colleagues]. He made it sound like I was lashing
out. I was under a lot of stress." Whatever stress he may have been
under at the time would have to be considered insignificant
compared to what followed: a national firestorm of controversy,
threats to him and his family, and the loss of his job.

David Mills, who now writes feature stories and music articles for the Washington Post, says this about the allegation he used chicanery to squeeze from Griff headline-grabbing quotes: "Griff's entitled to his opinion." (See the sidebar accompanying this article for relevant excerpts from the interview.) And like many reporters on the other end of an interview, Mills has a question of his own: "Why, in all this time, has nobody heard Griff speak on the substance of the question - whether he believed the things he said?" Here in Miami, Griff has now done that, and in recent days he's been less the professor and more the student.

At the time of the D.C. interview, Professor Griff held the post of 'Minister of Information' for the wildly popular rap group Public Enemy, formed in the mid-Eighties by current leader Chuck D and two college classmates in Long Island. Their 1987 debut LP, Yo! Bum Rush the Show, made an instant impression, both at the cash register (it sold more than 300,000 copies) and with music critics, mostly white music critics who abandoned their 'rap is not music' position as soon as Public Enemy introduced inflammatory political commentary to the genre. The rappers were mean and dangerous, unapologetically pro-black to the point, some suggested, that they were anti-white. Subsequently Public Enemy has become the most influential rap group since the major record labels (that is, mainstream America) discovered the music's marketability.

Griff wasn't so much a performer with the outfit at the time of the Mills interview as he was a behind-the-scenes contributor, and as 'Minister of Information' he had gained a reputation as Public Enemy's designated spokesman. By May of 1989, Public Enemy had attracted widespread attention with their album It Takes a Nation of Millions (To Hold Us Back), which sold well more than a million copies. Chuck D had become famous for his radical raps; sideman Flavor Flav for his goofy antics; and the group's gun-toting 'security force,' S1W (short for Security of the First World) for its intimidating presence. It was Griff who, in the formative days of Public Enemy, taught S1W members about martial arts and religious philosophy, much of the latter drawn from the ideology of Louis Farrakhan and the Nation of Islam.

47

Whatever reporter Mills interest in interviewing Griff, he came away with a hell of a tape-recorded conversation. Griff is articulate and engaging. He can't, however, count discretion among his virtues. If he has something on his mind, he soon has it on his lips. When that impulse comes into contact with controversial ideas (some of them borne of ignorance, Griff now admits), the results are often volatile.

Fallout from the Washington Times story was fast and fatal. After Mills piece was published, Griff says, "I was suspended by Public Enemy. Then I was fired. Hired. Fired again." Then Chuck D announced that his group was disbanding. Only later did he explain the reason for that drastic decision. One of Public Enemy's new songs, "Fight the Power," was being used in the Spike Lee film Do the Right Thing. Chuck D apparently wanted to save the movie's producers, and Spike Lee, the embarrassment of being associated with anti-Semitism.

The dissolution of the group didn't last long, however, and Griff seemed to be back in. But the public pressure on Public Enemy was too much. The Anti-Defamation League of B'Nai B'Rith protested to CBS/Columbia Records, which distributes Public Enemy's albums. Walter Yetnikoff, head of CBS, fired off a memo to his underlings demanding they pay more attention to what their acts were saying with regard to matters of ethnicity. Jewish leaders nationwide roundly condemned Griff's remarks, the national media went wild, and even former allies cut and ran. For example, Russell Simmons, co-founder of Public Enemy's record label, reportedly dismissed Griff as 'a racist stage prop.' By the end of last year, the Professor was gone for good from Public Enemy.

But if street talk is worth anything, he remained a threat to the group. In the heat of the fight, Griff told the press that certain anonymous individuals had approached him and volunteered assistance. These folks purportedly informed the Professor they'd gladly kill Chuck D and other offenders - free of charge. Griff says he declined, at least partially because he trusted Allah to deliver whatever vengeance was deemed worthy.

Today Griff says he just wants "peace," but clearly he remains bitter toward his former group. "There was no investigation," he says, "they had no right to speak. The majority of people [at the record labels] never heard what I said, nor did they just talk to me the way you're talking to me right now. They would rather fire me. That dollar, chump change - or Trump change, really - was being threatened. I feel sorry for Chuck. We grew up together and put Public Enemy together. And then I was fired over the phone, on TV and the newspapers. They just kicked me to the curb. And that's when my family was threatened."

In the year since the Washington Times article, Professor Griff has never publicly apologized for his anti-Semitic comments. But that changed dramatically last week, thanks in large part to a twenty-year-old Florida International University student named Sam Rogatinsky.

Three years ago Rogatinsky moved with his family from Houston to North Bay Village. While studying at FIU (he aspires to become an attorney), Rogatinsky grew concerned about the widespread lack of knowledge regarding Jewish history. Having attended the Hebrew Academy of Greater Miami, having lost family to the Holocaust, and having listened to his paternal grandparents describe in harrowing detail their survival in hiding during the Nazi atrocities (they were literally underground for years), Rogatinsky became convinced there simply "wasn't enough awareness." With an older brother and two friends, he formed the National Holocaust Awareness Student Organization, and began recruiting members. Today he serves as the group's president.

Rogatinsky is familiar with rap music. In fact, he likes it a great deal (he once interviewed Tone Loc for FIU's campus radio station), especially the hip-hop of Big Daddy Kane and, yes, even Public Enemy. But the furor that ensued after the publication of Griff's remarks overshadowed Rogatinsky's appreciation for the music. One day a few months ago, he recalls, he was at the Holocaust Memorial in Miami Beach when a group of students from an inner-city high school came through on a tour. He asked if he could say a few words to the visitors. "I asked them how many had heard of

Public Enemy. Their eyes lit up," he recounts. "Then I asked how many knew Professor Griff." Their eyes lit up again. I asked them how Professor Griff's comments about Jews made them feel. Nobody said much. A group of them came over to talk some more, and one kid said, "Griff's successful, he's been involved, so he must know what he's talking about. That one person was one too many."

When Rogatinsky learned that Professor Griff had signed a record contract with Miami's Luke Records, he saw an opportunity to take action. On April 13, he sent a letter to company president Luther Campbell. "We find it difficult to comprehend your recent acceptance of Professor Griff," Rogatinsky wrote. "He has repeatedly made cruel anti-Semitic remarks about Jewish people.... They are hurtful, malevolent, and contempt-filled." About a month later Rogatinsky wrote directly to Griff and requested an apology. He also mentioned that "both Jews and blacks face daily prejudices and injustices; therefore, it is difficult to comprehend any conflicts that exist between the two groups." After receiving the letter, Griff telephoned Rogatinsky and challenged the accuracy of Rogatinsky's interpretation. He also asserted that the media can twist reality into something ugly any time they please.

Late last week Professor Griff and Sam Rogatinsky met face-to-face for the first time. The setting was neutral territory - a photographer's studio in Miami Beach. Griff had dressed for the occasion: black hat, black shirt, black pants, black shoes, and a Luke Skywalker athletic jacket. Rogatinsky, the model student, wore a dress shirt, slacks, and brown penny loafers. Two more incongruous images of American youth could hardly be imagined. When they were introduced in the studio, Griff stood up to shake Rogatinsky's outstretched hand. "Wow!" Griff exclaimed. "I pictured you being taller, with glasses and graying hair." Rogatinsky, smiling, replied, "I pictured you much bigger." As photos were taken, the two launched into lively conversation:

Griff: "All that blacks know is that the Jews own everything, they're the bosses. Blacks know nothing about the history, and someone has to bridge that gap."

Rogatinsky: "How?"

Griff: "I have the vehicle - the music."

Rogatinsky: "Would Louis Farrakhan do it?"

Griff: "I believe he would. I need to get you tape of him meeting with rabbis. I use the means I have, you use the means you have, and we can bridge this gap. Give me the facts."

Rogatinsky: "You would do this?"

Griff: "Yes."

Rogatinsky: "I hate to think that blacks and Jews would be fighting each other. Our people both were enslaved. I understand what your people are going through."

Griff: "It's one big mess. But we don't need to be fighting each other."

Then Griff brightened and said to Rogatinsky, "This is a rarity. I mean, you're actually opening up to me."

Apparently, at one point, the two realized that the trouble with life in America isn't so much the result of ethnic differences as it is the trickle-down of a corrupt system. As the conversation turned to American politics, Rogatinsky asked Griff why he hasn't addressed that subject through his music. Griff seemed a bit confused by the question. That is one of the most prominent subjects of his debut album. A surprised Rogatinsky had to admit that he hadn't yet listened to the whole record.

After being forced to leave Public Enemy, Professor Griff went on to record what some critics, including the highly regarded Dave Marsh, consider a masterful rap album, Pawns in the Game. Last year Griff recruited five solo rappers with 'different styles, old and new, slow and fast.' He dubbed them the Last Asiatic Disciples, and

51

gave them stage names: Life, X, B-Wyze, Obie, and JXL. Though he lacked a recording contract, Griff began putting songs together at his Long Island studio, and in the fall, Griff signed a deal with Miami-based Skyywalker Records, now known as Luke Records, home of the notorious 2 Live Crew. Eighteen days later, Pawns in the Game was completed.

While it may be forever clouded by Griff's previous association with Public Enemy, the fact is Griff's album not only stands alone, but exposes Public Enemy's concurrent effort, Fear of a Black Planet, as a Pink-Floyd-meets-hip-hop jumble of nonsense. Where his former associates have lowered themselves to incorporating random sonic distractions, such as a seemingly interminable, self-referential montage of radio talk-show gibberish, Griff has crafted cutting songs that all but draw blood. If 'Pass the Ammo' is a scathing and melodic statement about young people deprived of education because they're too poor to afford tutors or nice-neighborhood private schools, 'Suzi Wants to Be a Rock Star' ups the ante on all of rap music. 'Suzi,' the LP's centerpiece, is not the most compelling drug-related rap song ever put to wax - it's the single most evocative drug-related song in any genre. It's a rock song with rap verses, and it lights a dozen thematic fires under the raging drug-abuse inferno. America, sings Griff, is a drug-sucking whore; crack is the throbbing currency of destruction. And beyond the impassioned and painful truths exposed in 'Suzi' is the sheer elegance of the song, its grand musical eloquence.

On January 19 Skyywalker released a statement. "Since Griff will be doing interviews, videos, and a tour, we hope this shows how strongly we stand behind him as an artist. Any beliefs, political or religious, are solely those of Professor Griff and the Last Asiatic Disciples. We want it clearly understood that [they] are part of the Skyywalker family based on their potential as artists."

Griff says now that he had offers from other labels, but came to Miami and Luke Records because the move offered him the freedom of expression he wanted. It's not paradise, though. "I really, really disagree with a lot of [the label's] points," he says. "But they told me, 'You do it as you see fit.'" Among the disagreements is the fact that Campbell's group, 2 Live Crew, sings humorously about sex and little else. Griff rarely mentions sex in his songs; each is a miniature political manifesto. (That should make for a startling contrast when the two groups begin a national tour together this week).

There's also the matter of the Crew's banned album As Nasty as They Wanna Be. "My daughter [six-year-old Taqiyyah] asked me why she couldn't listen to it," Griff says. "So I had to explain it to her, that its material made for adults. Listen, you can't go from first grade straight to sixth grade. That's the way I deal with it." In fact, raising the issue, Griff argues, can be beneficial if it leads to communication between parent and child. "It's better than if the kids learn it from movies or magazines or their peers."

If he switched positions with Luther Campbell and became president of the record label, Griff says he would sign the 2 Live Crew, as artists. We don't dive into each other's personal beliefs. We could go on about that for days. In a capitalistic society, you have to survive. Luke offers the whole spectrum with the artists on his label. I think conflict is good, and I know that I wouldn't fit in at many labels the way I fit in here. Despite his aversion to raunchy lyrics, Griff is vehemently opposed to artistic censorship. "I'm going on a college speaking tour," he says, "to talk about censor sh_t." When I give this talk, I'm going to point out the positive of rap as a communication vehicle to all ethnic groups. It's an international language, like a smile. You don't smile in Italian or Spanish or English. I'm going to explain their rights and that they have rights that they don't even know about. These parents who are trying to come down on this - well, if they don't know what little Johnny is listening to, that's really sad. On the cover of Griff's album are printed these words: "Explicit language contained. Parental discretion advised." However, cuss words are used sparingly and the sort of sex talk that landed 2 Live Crew in hot water is completely absent. Griff addresses matters of the intellect, not the genitals. If the album has a theme, it is contained in its title, Pawns in the Game. "Society plays out white supremacy," explains Professor

53

Griff. "Like pool - the white ball knocking the colors in. The last one on the table is black [i.e., the eight ball]. In chess, the pawns leave the board first. People up front are used as pawns first - AIDS, crack, ice remove them. It's just like Hitler's plan, which was aimed at the darker skinned and the Jews. The Hitler mentality still exists in a lot of people."

For Professor Griff knowledge is the strongest weapon in the human arsenal, though in the naiveté of youth (he refuses to reveal his age), he has been inclined to regurgitate the ideas of his heroes, particularly Louis Farrakhan. And that is at the root of his recent problems. Behind the desk in his new office at Luke Records in northeast Miami, Griff takes a cassette tape from one of several plastic milk crates filled with them. It's a speech by the Nation of Islam's Abdul Allah Muhammad, delivered November 17, 1985. The title typed on the tape's label reads, "Will the Real Jews Please Stand Up." From the verbiage on that tape came the name of Griff's group, the Last Asiatic Disciples, because Asia represents the 'whole world.' Also from that tape - as well as from various 'elders,' street acquaintances, and other sources - Griff received what he calls 'a lopsided view of the situation. I take this stuff in and it affects me.' In an ironic echo of the words Sam Rogatinsky heard from the youngster at the Holocaust Memorial, Griff adds, "I'm taking it from a tape by a man who is smarter, more articulate, better informed than I am. Don't put it all on me. And you know, I haven't run across too many Jews willing to talk it out." Rogatinsky himself changed that.

As the Miami Beach photo session concluded, a revealing reversal of roles occurred. Rogatinsky the student became a professor, and Griff the professor became a student. "If you have a question about Jewish history," Rogatinsky told Griff, "call me. If I don't know the answer, I'll find out who does for you." Griff in turn promised to fax a list of questions to Rogatinsky's organization. Then they jumped into Rogatinsky's green 1985 Volvo and drove the short distance to the Holocaust Memorial at Dade Boulevard and Meridian Avenue.

Rogatinsky acted as guide. "I explained to him what the pictures of the Holocaust were, about the human medical experiments," Rogatinsky said later. "I took him progressively through the memorial and into that tunnel to the statue. In the tunnel there's a skylight with the word 'Jude' on it. I explained they put that on badges and would make Jews wear them so they could pick them out on the street. We went through the tunnel and I showed him the statue. He didn't know about the tattooed numbers branded on their arms. He didn't know about that. I explained that this is fairly recent, only 40 or 50 years ago. Griff kept saying, 'This is critical.'"

The experience, Professor Griff said, was enlightening. "I saw things I wasn't aware of even after talking to my Jewish friends in New York," he admitted. "It was my first time experiencing anything like that. Black kids don't know these things. I study, and I didn't know about some of these things, so the black kids without education definitely don't know about them." "I had mixed emotions - both sad and angry," Griff continued. "It made me think! If that happens to them, if six million people can have that happen to them, imagine the 250 million blacks. It could happen to them, too. I mentioned to Sam that I bet a lot of Jewish people don't come here, because I know that if I was Jewish, I couldn't take seeing this. And he told me that, yes, that for some Jews it was too painful."

The following day Griff reflected further on his encounter with Sam, the Holocaust Memorial, and his own notorious words of a year ago. "I'm just sad about the whole incident," he said in reference to the Washington Times interview. "I'm not even going to go back and single out the quotes I made. That's nothing compared to what I saw yesterday. Now I'm more angry about the whole shebang, to be honest with you. If I knew what I know now, I never would have uttered those words. I would have stayed away from whole subject."

But how would he reconcile his new historical perspective with his allegiance to the Nation of Islam? Suppose Louis Farrakhan himself called after reading these words and insisted that Griff had been taken in by some clever Jewish trick? "I don't think that would ever happen," said Griff. "He wouldn't say that. Now, someone in the

Nation would probably say that, and I would ask them to prove it. The thing is, this wickedness is not sanctioned on either side. The difference in religions is up to each individual. The Nation was built on truth and righteousness, and it doesn't mock human suffering. So I can empathize with Jews and sympathize with blacks at the same time."

"One thing about me is I'm not that kind of hollow person," he continued. "You can't figure me out in one or two conversations. I'm no politician and I'm no Chuck D. I don't talk in circles, I talk directly. If you think I was joking or kidding or putting up a front when I went to the memorial with the gentleman, well, we'll see. My views change with time, and my views about this have changed. This could be a process of me maturing."

As the two men were departing the Holocaust Memorial, Rogatinsky looked into Griff's clear brown eyes and said, "I'd like to be your friend." Griff recalled his answer: "I told him I'd love that. That we could try to do this together. That's not about trying to clear the way for me to make safe records, no. But he and I are young and sincere. I have a lot of energy and I'm ready and raring to go. You have to remember that a lot of prophets and messengers of God didn't even know what their mission was until it was revealed to them by God when these people were at a late age."

And then Samuel Rogatinsky and Richard Griffin shook hands.

1990 Luke SkyWalker Records

CHAPTER FOUR

BINDING BACK

Public Enemy Rap Group Reorganizes After Anti-Semitic Comments New York Times by JON PARELES Friday, August 11, 1989

Public Enemy, a rap group whose disbandment had been announced by its record company in the wake of anti-Semitic statements by its designated "Minister of Information," is "back in action," according to a statement released by the group on Wednesday.

Public Enemy's third album, "Fear of a Black Planet," is to appear this winter, and two of its three performing members - the rapper William (Flavor Flav) Drayton and the disk jockey Norman (Terminator X) Rogers - are also working on solo albums. Chuck D. Ridenhour is the group's songwriter and main rapper. One of Public Enemy's songs, "Fight the Power," is on the soundtrack of Spike Lee's new film, "Do the Right Thing," and a home video of the group, "Fight the Power Live," has just been released.

Controversy around the band began after Richard Griffin, formerly Public Enemy's minister of information, said in an interview with The Washington Times: "The Jews are wicked. And we can prove this." Mr. Griffin, who was known in the group as Professor Griff, also said that Jews are responsible for "the majority of wickedness that goes on across the globe." Group Member Dismissed June 21

At a news conference on June 21, Mr. Ridenhour announced the dismissal of Mr. Griffin, who did not perform or write songs but appeared on stage with the band as a member of the group's uniformed "security force." A few days later, Public Enemy's disbandment was announced by its record company, Def Jam.

Now, the band has reappeared. "I never said we disbanded," Mr. Ridenhour said in a telephone interview yesterday. "I said Griff had to lose his position."

Mr. Griffin, however, has been rehired by Public Enemy as the band's "supreme allied chief of community relations," the statement said, adding that "his duties will include service to the black community with special attention to local youth programs." Community Service Work

Mr. Ridenhour said Mr. Griffin will work with "programs of various organizations in the community like the Urban League, and work out personal appearances" such as performances, seminars or autograph signings. The band has a new minister of information, James Norman.

"Griff's statements were wrong and I apologized," Mr. Ridenhour said. "He also apologized to me. Griff wasn't clear in his thinking and he wasn't 100 per cent right. He's not going to make those statements any more, and he won't do interviews. He's definitely going to talk - you can't tell any man to be quiet, this is America - but he won't be dealing with any kind of major media. He's going to tell black kids to be the best they can be."

Mr. Ridenhour said Public Enemy did not intend to be divisive, but to urge self-development for the black community. "The problem is the system of white world supremacy," he said. "It's not white people, but the system that benefits them more than us. And the counterattack for black people is intelligence, self-sufficiency and self-development. You have to build a respect mechanism for yourself, as a self-defense mechanism, and make yourself as strong a person as you can possibly be."

1987 London

The Return of Professor Griff

An interview with Public Enemy's controversial Minister of
Information Creative Loafing Published 06.12.02 By Roni Sarig

In 1989, revolutionary black-power hip-hop group Public
Enemy was in the midst of its greatest stretch of music
making. Then in May of that year, *The Washington Times* quoted
P.E.'s non-performing Minister of Information, Professor Griff
(Richard Griffin), as saying "the majority of [Jews]" are responsible
for "the majority of wickedness that goes on across the globe," and
other anti-Jewish statements. In the media storm that ensued, Griff
was kicked out of the group and, for a short time, P.E. broke up
entirely. They were soon back, though, and years later, Griff was
quietly welcomed back into the P.E. fold, where he remains.

While he largely disappeared from public consciousness in 1989,
Griff released a number of solo albums during the 1990s. More
recently, he's given lectures on "hip-hop and revolution" in Atlanta,
where he now lives, and is working on a hip-hop children's music
project, Hip-hop Kids Biz. Griff led a Hip-hop Town Hall Meeting
in Atlanta during Hip-hop Appreciation Week in late May.

Creative Loafing: **At the town hall meeting, you said, "No one would
sign me after that quote unquote Jewish comment." That's referring
to the [incident from 1989]?**

Professor Griff: Right, I know exactly what I was referring to. I can't
give it to you in this conversation, simply because I'd have to go
back and give you documented history before I repeat that
statement. Because that ni--r took that comment out of context.

61

How was it taken out of context?

Like I said, I'd have to explain the history and give the historical research behind it, and then give you the comment that was made. And that, I'm not willing or able to do.

Under what circumstances would you do that?

If we had a couple of armed guards [laughs], and the conversation was recorded with some Jewish people and some black people there that we respected. Because the last time I had a conversation like this, it ended up in a sh_t storm. And it's really sad.

So the quote that got into the press, do you stand by it?

No, I can't stand by something taken out of context. If I said to you, "Nelly needs to respect hip-hop history." And you write, "Professor Griff said Nelly needs his ass whipped," that's on you, bro. And you might get the ass whipping, because you're writing something I never said.

So you never said those words that came out?

Exactly. How that guy twisted that thing up to make me sound like I was condemning people, that's bad.

So you were not condemning anyone?

No, definitely not. I was stating historical facts.

What historical facts?

Like I said, I have historical documents backing what I say up.

So you have historical documents proving Jews are responsible for the majority of wickedness in the world?

I never said that, and I'm not lending any credence to that statement at all.

How much has this thing affected your career?

Wooh! F_ck a career. That affected my whole life. Physically got poisoned, got ostracized. Now to a certain degree, I'm hated by black people; I'm hated by other people. That's not cool, bro. Just for some ni--r taking my words out of context.

So there was nothing about it that you regret?

I think it was probably the manner in which it was presented. Right now, me and you are talking, and if I get excited or express certain points, grammatically it might not come out the way it should have. The way I say it and the way you write it are two different things, right?

No, I'm going to write exactly what you say.

Well, I wish David Mills would've done that. If he had, you and I wouldn't be having this conversation right now.

So can you answer yes or no, do you feel that Jews were responsible for the majority of wickedness...?

I can't answer yes or no to that simply because it's a statement I never made.

I'm not asking if you said it, I'm asking right now, do you feel that way?

No, that's f_cking foolish, I don't believe that. And I told them that then. Even if we just took the word wickedness and defined it, then went all across the globe to see who was at the bottom of all the wickedness, you're not going to find Jewish people. There's all kinds of people. So how could I lend something to that statement?

Boston, Mass 2004

ONE-on-ONE: A Conversation
with Professor Griff

by FinalCall.com News
Updated Oct 26, 2004 - 7:13:00 AM

Often controversial and never one to hold his tongue, Professor Griff spoke with Final Call Online Correspondent Ashahed Muhammad.

Final Call (FC): First of all, it's good talking to you after all of this time. What types of things are you involved in right now?

Professor Griff (PG): The one thing that takes precedence is I am involved in the next Sesame Street, but with a hip hop theme. I created a theme called Kid Hoppaz. I designed some characters that actually do rap songs and speak to some of the things that children need in their growing stages. We deal with certain themes in the songs. We wrote stories and we're trying to bring it to life as far as doing live shows and ultimately a television program.

FC: How did that idea originate?

PG: It originated basically with me driving back and forth from North Carolina to Atlanta with my children in the backseat, listening to them sing songs that they hear on the radio. There's no real music out there for children. You look for music for children, especially Black children, you would definitely have to go to music that White people make, that's catered towards and that deals with subjects that their children may deal with, and arrange it in a way that our children would understand these things.

Basically, what I did was, I just put stories and I put lessons to music. We learn in rhythmic patterns anyway, so I just took a subject like "Respect"—"Respect your parents," "Respect yourself," you know, "Respect everyone around you" and just put it in a song form on a level in which two to seven-year-olds can understand, but in a real kind of way.

FC: CD and audio tape, or are you going video with it? Is it going to be on television?

PG: I wrote the stories, wrote the songs, recorded them, designed the characters, got a video production that I'm working with, got an illustrator that I'm working with and we're trying to bring it to life, for ultimately video and DVD.

FC: I heard that you had a new album coming out.

PG: I finished my last album about four months ago. I have an album that's coming out, called The 7th Degree, with a band I put together called the 7 Octaves. I got tired of rapping over the loops and beats and the drum machines. I just took it live. Not only that, my last album came out in 2001, September 11.

FC: "The Word Became Flesh."

PG: Right. The album after that was the "Revolverlution" album, with Public Enemy, and that was July 2003. So, there's material out there. A lot of times, you know, with us, if it ain't in our face on TV, BET or MTV or on the radio, people will run into you and ask you, "So, what you been doing? I haven't heard from you in a while." But it's actually out there. I've done a couple of songs for a couple of movies. I've done a couple of songs for some video games.

FC: In your lyrics, you always inject much-needed consciousness into the minds of the listening public. Most music, in general, is

lacking any type of material for your brain, and with hip hop in particular, that is also a problem. What has kept you from going the easy commercial route even if it means that the major distributors might stay away from you, resulting in lower record sales?

PG: Having come into the music industry with the knowledge of self and being a Muslim in the Nation, it's like, there's just certain things that are already instilled and in place with you, that you can't feed your people on the physical level, but on the spiritual level. And I know and understand that the airways are sacred. I do believe in karma and that stuff, that kind of stuff comes back.

I'm not going to be foolish enough to get on the airways and write a song and use my pen to write some foolishness and then hope for the chance that this stuff gets out and reaches the ears of young people and destroys the spirit in them and destroys their minds. That's death and destruction. I don't want any part of that. I don't care how much these cats are getting paid. I believe in something a whole lot higher than the music industry or than a few fans and some chump change. I know and understand that I've got to go before the Lord of the Worlds in the Last Day and I know I'm not going to be able to explain that. I refuse to lend my talents that were given to me by the Creator to put some filth out, some nonsense.

FC: What do you think is the biggest challenge facing hip hop today in becoming more culturally relevant, other than making people buy Hennessey or making people buy this particular type of watch or trying to drive a certain type of car?

PG: I think the biggest challenge is them actually facing a devil, in which The Honorable Elijah Muhammad always taught us, truly exists. When you've got to meet and deal with a real God and a real devil, while you're living, that's much (more) difficult to do. These guys don't figure that there's going to be no direct punishment for this. As long as you don't say anything positive for your people, to uplift the conscious level of your people, the devil will leave you alone and reward you. Which is sad, and I think we need to understand this, I call it "hidden in plain sight." It's almost an unspoken kind of thing nowadays, in the music industry. If you talk about negativity, if you deal in negativity, keep your people deaf, dumb and blind, the devil will reward you. Then, we've got conscious people who are in key positions that won't even say anything.

FC: Several months ago in Atlanta, you were there when Minister Farrakhan recently spoke. He was supposed to speak at Morris Brown and because of pressure from outside forces, the venue was moved to the Hyatt, and it was still packed with an enthusiastic crowd. Minister Farrakhan addressed reparations and the inordinate control over the education of Black students. What are your thoughts?

PG: Rally up the forces, talk to other hip hop artists about at least pushing the reparations agenda before the hip hop community, therefore pushing it before the world, because hip hop is global. It was that spirit that the Minister had that "Public Enemy" used to take and put in the songs, because that was our core.

If (we) weren't linked and plugged into the Nation, how do people think that we did this? This was done with the spirit of the F.O.I. and the M.G.T., the spirit of the Minister, the Spirit of Allah, and galvanizing that energy and putting it into the writing and the production with our people in mind.

So, what I heard in the Minister that Saturday was almost, "Ok, this is going to be a fight. And if you're not prepared to take on this fight, it's best for you to just back up, put your little cheerleading skirt on, and just move to the side." I think this is going to separate the wheat from the tare, the strong from the weak. Those that really want to be in this struggle, because we fought for other things, a whole lot less important than reparations. And we've been beat, killed, water-hosed, dogs sicced on us, lynched, falsely accused and imprisoned, for less. If you take up the fight for Black people in reference to reparations, we're in a fight, man.

FC: There's a lot of people, around that period of time in the late 1980s, early 1990s when we first saw Professor Griff and the S1W, all the conscious rappers like Lakim Shabazz, Big Daddy Kane, Rakim, Brand Nubian, The Jungle Brothers. When you saw the women, they still had their fezzes on and they were covered up and dressed and it was on a different level. Now, you've got these people just basically naked on TV. Do you think change will come externally from the artists or is it something that the people, the listening public, is going to have to say, "We're not standing for this anymore. We're no longer going to buy this, so you'll have to change the lyrics."

PG: I think it has to happen two-fold, Brother. I think the makers of the songs and the listening audience, we both have to do it simultaneously. We have to just say, listen, at least the Brothers inside of the music industry that know have to educate the Brothers that don't know and just put a certain amount of pressure on these Brothers. It doesn't take much. It takes a little bit of studying, something that they may not want to do.

FC: Thank you.

2007 San Diego

Unity Force

Art Voice 3/2008 by Geoff Kelly

Public Enemy's Professor Griff comes to Buffalo next week to lecture at the Freedom Film Festival

It's been a cruel winter for Professor Griff: Last month a gas leak caused his house and studio in Atlanta to burn down. He and his family lost everything—clothes and valuables, book and record collections, lectures, studio equipment, the artifacts and memorabilia collected over the course of a career that reaches back more than 20 years.

Griff's most famous role in that long career is minister of communications for Public Enemy, the pioneering hip-hop revolutionaries fronted by his childhood friend, Chuck D. But Griff (born Richard Griffin) has made his own name in the world as well, separate from but always in pursuit of the same agenda that drove Public Enemy: empowering black people, countering media dissembling, fighting the powers that be.

Griff comes to town next Thursday and Friday to deliver a lecture and screen the documentary he helped to make last year, *Turn Off Channel Zero*, which deals with the African-American stereotypes that populate the dominant American media. The film is part of Morningstar Promotion's Freedom Film Festival, which takes place March 21 & 22 at the Screening Room (in the Northtown Plaza, 3131 Sheridan Drive). Other filmmakers include Doug Ruffin, Jr. and Karima Amin of Prisoners Are People Too, Kameran Woods and Andrew P. Mitchell. (The program runs 6-10pm both days, and Griff's lecture is on Friday evening; check myspace.com/morningstarpromotions for more details.) Professor Griff took time this week to talk to Artvoice about *Turn Off Channel Zero*, among other things:

Artvoice: How did you become involved with *Turn Off Channel Zero*?

Griff: Opio Sokoni was at the Black Holocaust Conference in D.C., and listening to all the speakers speak, it came to him that in order for us to balance this all out and to produce the next group of black leaders that are going to come up and speak on behalf of black people, young black students need to see strong black men.

And we're just not seeing this. When we went to go find them, the majority of them had been bought off by this government, co-opted. They don't really speak black, they don't speak for black people. This is a problem, because we don't see ourselves in the educational system. I mean, when you start talking about Little Black Sambo and Ten Little Niggers—these were books that were being used to educate black people. It's not healthy. We could not find a strong black man.

And then the whole aspect of the feminization of the African male. It's ridiculous: Every strong black male figure that goes to Hollywood has to put on a dress, with the exception of Dave Chappelle and Denzel Washington. Dave Chappelle turned down $50 million, just to say, "No, I'm not doing it," and we don't know what Denzel Washington turned down. But you can't find too many black men in Hollywood that didn't put on the dress.

AV: So you've made this film, to talk about and expose that.

Griff: Yeah, we've brought it to the forefront. Being that hip-hop was so prevalent with young people, we tried to balance it out, and say, "Where are the strong black male images in hip-hop?" It was very, very difficult to find them?

72

AV: In regard to the perpetuation of old stereotypes and the creation of new ones, how have things changed in that regard since you and Public Enemy first came onto the scene? Do you think the atmosphere is better or worse?

Griff: I think there was a period of rise and fall, of hills and valleys. I think when Public Enemy, when we were at our peak, I think we had raised the consciousness level of the people to the point where those who were playing this kind of trickery and this kind of game had to go back and reassess some of their strategy.

And they did! They just started outright paying people large sums of money to do the madness that they do: i.e. *Flavor of Love*; i.e. gangsta rap; i.e. Snoop Dogg. You understand what I'm saying? And now we no longer look at it like a badge of shame. We look at it as a badge of honor. It's cool to be dumb and ignorant.

AV: At the height of Public Enemy's popularity, there were other African-American musical acts and filmmakers who were not being socially conscious, who were not contributing to a revolution or cause. Is that okay? Does every African-American artist have to be socially conscious?

Griff: Oh, absolutely not. There are beautiful brothers and sisters, Doug E. Fresh is one of them who I'm close friends with. He's the greatest entertainer in hip-hop. Does he have to be socially conscious and politically aware, *outside* of the context of hip-hop? I would think so. The community and our culture need to hold him accountable for some of the things he says, because he has influence over the people, inside his music. Can we have fun, just have fun? Can you and I hang out this Saturday and just have fun, without discussing a whole lot politically? Yes. We need that, because we need the balance.

But now let's look at the scales, how they're lopsided. Ninety-nine point nine percent of the artists that entertain us, and black people in movies, just disrespect black people blatantly. And disrespect themselves, and that's sad. No other people on the planet will allow that. Not Indians, from India; they have too much pride. Japanese, Chinese, Jewish Americans...no one will allow that. No one has 99.9 percent of their artists making records and doing things in films that disrespect their people.

AV: So where do black people today find positive images, or find images at least that aren't destructive?

Griff: I think we need a roadmap. You know how you go to Hollywood and you get those roadmaps to the stars? We need to develop a roadmap, because it is truly, truly, truly sad. It's almost at a point where—

AV: Whose houses are on that map? Wesley Snipes? Is his house on the map?

Griff: Aw, you're out of your mind. You could do a history of his films—wow. That dude dressed up as a woman? Wow. That's critical. But, no. I think we would have to stop by Barack Obama's house first.

AV: What do you think about Obama's public image? What is the image that he's projecting to white and black audiences?

Griff: To young people, he is giving a glossy image of presenting himself, or being presented by the people that control him, as the next Kennedy, the next Dr. King, you know. That's the way he is being presented and propped up. Personally speaking, I think he's connected to the bluebloods, and you know if you have that bloodline you're not going to be the president of the United States of America. We know that. We know how many of them were related to one another. We know the blueblood line, we know the secret society, because it's our people. We know this information because it's out there. It's no secret now. It's not about what you know, whether or not you're the best man or woman for the job. We know who you have to be connected to, in order to preserve this status quo, so to speak.

The reality of it when it comes to young people, especially black people, seeing a black man running for the highest office in the land, it just swells their chests for some reason with pride. Just trying to see us through another four or five years...It's a false hope, but nonetheless it's still hope.

AV: Why do you say a false hope?

Griff: Simply because you and I both know the day they say that he's the President of the United States, you know he's on the list for assassination. You know this. Once they open up those files in the back room...once he utters the fact that he might sign into law the reparations bill, to pay black people back...

AV: You think Barack Obama's going to do that?

Griff: Hell, no. You know that. But the thought of it, you understand? I heard on the news the other day that the white conservatives are talking about, "It's going to be a problem because his middle name is 'Hussein,' and al Qaeda's actually going to think it's a victory for them." Which is wildly crazy, it's insane for them to even think that they're going to win the guy as president. Because he's president on face value, but the policies are not necessarily going to change. The presidency is a public seat; there's someone else pulling those strings. We know that. Can we put this in the paper, in the article? Probably not. [*He laughs.*] You've got to keep your job.

AV: You'd be surprised what we can put in our paper.

Griff: Oh, I hear you.

AV: We can get away with a lot.

Griff: Isn't that something that you and I have to use that language? "We can get away with a lot"? Ain't that something?

AV: Well, it used to be that you had to be worried about whatever vehicle it was you used to communicate; you had to worry about keeping it alive, which meant making compromises. Do you feel that technology has changed your ability to communicate, to reach out, to be an activist?

Griff: It's a blessing and a curse. It's a blessing simply because right now you and I can have this conversation, and in the next five minutes we can have it out throughout the world. Literally. But false information can be put out about you and I—that we're gay, that we're secretly lovers—that can also go out, and it can also damage your career and mine. So it's a blessing and a curse. We can get information out instantaneously, but who we reach and how we reach them is [determined by] the medium that someone else set up, as far as Google, Yahoo, Gmail, Hotmail, all this other stuff. We have to go through their medium.

But then again, who can afford, who actually has access to computers? And once the average 17-, 18-year-old logs in, where are they going? What chat rooms, what communities, what blogs? So it's still a challenge; we still have to find what's attractive to them. That's our job.

You see, hip-hop had no script; it was organic. It went out, and for the most part white people didn't know what the hell we were talking about. They didn't know "a-hip, a-hop, the hippy, the hippy to the hop," they didn't know what that was. Once we started validating, and they started validating and packaging hip-hop, then it became the curse. We sold out to the highest bidder.

AV: So where is that sort of cultural secret now? Where is that thing that only black people have now? Is there something like that, like hip-hop as it was back then?

Griff: Well, my thing is, even now, when we discuss certain things, in the way we discuss them, and the trends and the fashion and the talk and the swagger, and what we listen to and how we listen to it and how we interact with it—I think that being the people that we are, we invite every other people in, every other culture in. And it's critical because in any given black movement, in any given black trend, there's only X number of white people that come in. But with hip-hop, oh my God...

And we don't mind. But the curse is that they co-opted it, corrupted it, turned it into something else. Dumbed it down for mass consumption.

AV: Is there any hope for hip-hop out there? Are there any artists or any groups out there that are doing something that you can respect? Some new direction?

Griff: Oh, you and I know there's nothing new under the sun. But I love Lupe Fiasco and what he's doing. Immortal Technique, NY Oil, Jean Grae...these artists will probably never get the Grammys and the awards like Lupe Fiasco received, but these artists are bubbling under. They're really moving underground. There still is an underground—you have to really submerge extra deep, because this stuff that's considered underground is not really underground; it's really pop. Underground has no rules, no holds barred. You just go for it.

AV: And that's where music changes.

Griff: Exactly, exactly. Now you can't differentiate between what they're calling underground and what's above the ground. Its like, "That sounds like something that should be on the radio." That's not cool; we ain't checking for that. I was in the club the other night and they were playing some stuff and I was like "Who was that?" and they were like, "These artists don't even want you to know who they are." The guy just made this in his bedroom two weeks ago, and that's the kind of stuff you see on YouTube.

But you're also seeing 16-, 18-year-old girls taking off their clothes on YouTube. And it's like, wow, this is critical. You have to guard your children from it, at the same time you've got to be on there to get the information. Blessing and a curse.

AV: So, what's next for you? What are you working on now, besides a new house?

Griff: [*He laughs.*] I'm glad we can kind of chuckle about it.

AV: I'm sorry to laugh...

Griff: No, I need to. I need a laugh. I am trying to finish my book, *The Psychological Covert War on Hip-Hop.*

AV: Tell me about that.

Griff: The whole idea is to try to uncover this covert war that's going on in this genre of music, of black music that we call hip-hop. And there is a war going on. For example, in the book *The First Millennium Edition of the American Directory of Certified Uncle Toms*, on page 236 it talks about the nefarious negroization of hip-hop, rap music... [They] created this certain tone that they call the Twelve Atonal Tones, [which] they've put among hip-hop and actually made this thing, created this thing called gangsta rap. Put it among our people and paid gangsta rappers large sums of money to carry these frequencies, this tone, throughout hip-hop. We see the end result, and it worked. They created gangsta rap to neutralize conscious hip-hop, i.e., created NWA to neutralize Public Enemy.

If I ran down a list of all the young white independent record company owners who took instructions from their forebears that said, "We have to keep this thing going, and get paid from it. They want to kill themselves, dope and crack and sing about it, then we'll profit off of it." It's a fascinating story.

But we were the first targets; you have to understand that. Starting with Public Enemy.

AV: Were you aware of that at the time?

Griff: No, not at all. There's a gentleman who wrote a book called *Hip-Hop Decoded*, and his name is The Black Dot, and it really opened my eyes. And then Congresswoman Cynthia McKinney pointed things out to me that were just mindblowing...[she] gave me documents showing that we were under surveillance, that black rap and hip-hop artists were under surveillance. I went to go look into it, thinking that, okay, I'll find one article, maybe two. I started uncovering document after document after document, not only on myself and Public Enemy but just the average artists—hell, Chingy. Chingy? I'm like, he's the cutest little guy in music, man. What is he threatening? You know if they've got a file on his ass, you know what they have on me.

Seriously—they don't want strong black intelligent men in the industry, that's not going to sell out, that's actually going to do right by the people. Some white people look at this, they say, "Well, if he's doing right and making a sacrifice by his people, we ain't got nothing to worry about." But there are some segments of the human family that's not looking at it like that. They looking at this thing like, "Griff is a threat. Public Enemy is a threat. We can't have too many Public Enemy groups out there like that."

AV: That was the thing about Public Enemy: It didn't end after a concert, or after a CD comes out. You guys are were lecturing, you were going out in the community—

Griff: Right, right.

AV: You're like any activist group. Who does that now?

Griff: Talib Kweli, Mos Def. On a different level, you know—it's not the same tenacity. They don't do it with the same dignity and the same passion. They do Cadillac commercials and beer commercials, which is not going to get it; that's not going to get it.

AV: That's not a radical message, for sure.

Griff: Desperate times call for desperate measures. One breath you're telling kids to just do this, that or the other, but you're

79

profiting off of their misery by making a beer commercial. That's counterproductive. It's counterrevolutionary.

1987 Def Jam Records NYC

Breakdown FM- Part 1

The History of Public Enemy August 20, 2007
Davey D- Moderator (DD)
Professor Griff- Guest Speaker (PG)

DD: Sitting in front of me is the one and only legendary Minister of Information from the world's greatest rap group, one of the greatest music groups of all times celebrating their 20th anniversary. We are down here in the City of Angels, Los Angeles. We are here with the one and only Professor Griff. How are you doing family?

PG: I am doing okay man, feeling the nice weather and my heart and soul is rocking and reeling with the passing the good Baba, Asa Hilliard. Egyptologist, Historian, good brother. It is kind of critical man it's just a different kind of energy in the air.

DD: I was going to ask you about that. For people who are not familiar, let's lace them up as to who Asa Hilliard is, why he is so important and why there would be a lot of people around with heavy hearts. Because you know, at the same time a lot of people do not know who he is.

PG: Well, I think, simply because when you talk about a brother who stood up fighting to actually change and introduce certain things into the curriculum in the educational system in the United States of America and what he wanted to bring was the whole aspect of Kemetology. Not Egyptology, the whole study of Kemet, the whole study of melanin, the whole study of the dynasties that was here long before any people were thought of. And this brother fought so hard to

82

do these things and wrote books on curriculum change you know.

DD: It is interesting, when you talk about, when you made the separation it seems like what we are talking about is this resistance to really allow people of Nubian descent have their rightful place in history. To acknowledge the genius of a people, who have been enslaved and marginalized and put into a position where people go "They needed to be civilized." It is ironic that we were the civilizing force in terms of creating the sciences and mathematics that are used. But the way that the history books would have you believe today is that we were the people that were in need of so much help, and we were the ones that need to be uplifted and needed to be taught.

PG: Right. This is why it is so very important that Asa Hilliard, his body of work, the other people that he's affected because it is not just that you are doing your work when you put your work out, you give birth to other individuals. There is a circle of people that he operated among, very brilliant brothers and sisters, and those who are unfamiliar with Asa Hilliard's work; you know we have the Internet now. We can put his name in the search engine and at least you know 200 pages will come up.

DD: We have to make sure it is the right one because you have people who are trying to undermine. But some of the other people, there was a trilogy of scientist and folks who really played key roles in redefining, really bringing up that history. One of course, Asa Hilliard, the other one is Dr. Ben and the Cheikh Anta Diop.

PG: Cheikh Anta Diop and Dr. John Henry Clarke.

DD: That is right, four. Four, I'm sorry there is four.

PG: But we cannot forget Runoko Rashidi, we cannot forget Ash Ra Kwese and his wife Mary Ra-Kwase (check spelling). We cannot forget Ivan Van Sertima. I could call the roll; Professor Smalls, Professor Simmons, Professor James, Dr. Lenard Jeffries, Shaun McIntire, I could go on and on, but these are the people that are walking among us. These are greats that are walking among us and we act as though they didn't lay their lives out to put together a body of work, so that we could at least remember. Are you following me? Not implementing it in the educational system, these brothers and sisters are here to prick our conscious so we could even remember that we were a great people and that greatness still lies within our genetic code. And it is up to brothers like you and I to stand on their shoulders and unlock those genetic keys and stuff that is locked in our genetic code, to say, for young brothers like those sitting across from us that they don't ever feel the effect of getting mis-educated because brothers that went before us and did the work.

DD: We are talking to Professor Griff as we celebrate the 20th anniversary of Public Enemy. We were talking off air and you were saying that there is some strange dynamics going on. The fact that we lost some very key elders; Asa Hilliard and of course, we lost Chauncey Bailey, Darryl Jones and then at the same time we have ---well, you describe it. The type of ravaging going on with the human resources in our communities.

PG: Well, you know something, our greatest resource and we don't know it or not, now we need to know it, and whether we know it or not our greatest resource is our natural genius. Some people may have material wealth, our greatest resource is that natural energy that we have and that natural energy is being used in different areas and most cases used against us. We need to harness that energy that we have and put it towards something that is going to work for us as a whole, collectively. Not just for individuals. You know, this is the me-me-me, I-I-I society. It's all about me, all the wealth that I can amass so that I can be something. Are you following me? We need to do away with that particular concept.

DD: How would it manifest itself in practical terms? Give us some ways in which you would see your vision operating.

PG: Those lines between the Haves and the Have-nots would be very, very blurry. The whole idea of some people being able to have access to certain resources, that would be a thing of the past because everyone, I think Zap Delaroche from

Raging At the Machine said it better "Everything for Everyone and nothing for ourselves.

DD: Mmm. That is real thought right there. We have been talking with Professor Griff. We are going to take a break and come back on the 20th anniversary of Public Enemy.

DD: We are back here. We have been talking with Professor Griff. We are down here in Los Angeles, California and you guys are here for an entire week. You know, and being on the West coast this is one of the areas that was really responsible for helping break Public Enemy in a big way. The Bay area and Los Angeles. In particular a legendary radio station out here KDAY played a big role. It is kind of ironic, that 20 years later, here you are in Los Angeles and you did the Jimmie Kimble show, headlined the Rock Bells tour getting ready to go down to San Diego be one of the headliners there, that very same radio station, which has now changed hands and moved on into a corporate stratosphere won't even let you on the air. Aint that something?

PG: That is not only ironic, that's just part of the neutralization of Public Enemy.

DD: Let me repeat this for people. 20 year anniversary, you are headlining everywhere; House of Blues, Public Enemy, a lot of information and wisdom to be shared. You have Flava Flav, if you don't want to have the seriousness of Chuck and Griff, is on TV every day. He just had high ratings for his roast. We have you and Chuck who are about... everybody knows you all around these communities on the West coast of all things. So they don't let you in the door to celebrate this landmark achievement of having a rap group, a group of brothers who can demonstrate to the world how you stay together and how you do things together and work it out even when you have some very challenging problems as you guys have had over your 20 year tenure. That is not allowed to be shared on the airwaves that talk and speak to the masses of our people in an area that in the same day we have gang violence and we need guidance. How does this happen?

PG: I think it happens as you said it earlier this is one of the places where it broke Public Enemy, now let's analyze that.

It broke Public Enemy, but it broke Public Enemy if you get what I am saying.

DD: Break it down for us.

PG: In the book "The First Millennium Edition of the Directory of Certified Uncle Toms" on page 236 it deals with the nefarious niggerization of Hip-Hop via the VIBE magazine and other magazines and other people. One of the first groups to come out of this experiment was NWA. NWA was kind of set up and used, good brothers, very political first coming out, f_ck the Police is very political. We understand they were quote, unquote keeping it real talking about what is going on in the streets and they gave us a vivid picture of what is going on. Beautiful thing, but the brothers were used to neutralize Public Enemy. Here I am, and here we are in Los Angeles today, after Flava Flav's roast yesterday. Public Enemy has been successfully neutralized to the point where those political, hard-core statements that were coming from the music and were coming from outside the context of the music, the people don't feel the sting of it anymore. Are you following me? Because, it's funny, you say after 20 years the same radio station that helped break us, helped break us because they won't even have us on the air. Are you following me? See, this is by design, this is the Plan. They did not write us into the Plan 20 years later. You understand what I am saying? They did not expect you at this time. Are you following me? Even with what you went through in your personal life having the trials and tribulations with radio stations and magazines, and the introduction of the Internet and what you are doing now, they didn't expect you 20 years later. Are you following me? That is deep in and of itself when you are talking about the psychological, covert war and raging war against our culture. They didn't expect you to be doing what you are doing. We didn't expect that we would be sitting here with this.

DD: Talking about my digital recorder. But, now having a national audience to reach this point.

PG: Exactly. You told me the other day, this is one of the things Public Enemy was at the forefront of.

DD: Let's go back in the time for this. It is interesting, because we started talking about history with Asa Hilliard and how he fought to really bring keen understanding to the concept of Kemet. I don't know if concept is the right word, but the reality of Kemet, that whole civilization, the whole culture that surround it.

PG: There would be no American culture if it was not for Kemetic culture.

DD: But we also said there are generations of young brothers and sisters that don't know who Asa Hilliard is, and this is by design that this morning he passes and I can listen to various radio shows here with black host and playing black music and he is not talked about. Whether it is from Steve Harvey on down that we are still having battle of the sexes, and other things and maybe even a conversation of whether or not Lindsay Lowan will get out of rehab before we talk about...let's take a time out and talk about Asa Hilliard. The connection to what we were talking about with Public Enemy and not understanding history and the significance is that a lot of the things we do today with modern technology, one of the things that people don't recognize is that Public Enemy as a group-above and beyond just you and Chuck and Flav -- were pioneers in that regard. Let me share some history; Harry Allen, who was your first publicist, media sass and hip-hop held a conference in 1991, let's go back, let's digest that. In 1991 Harry Allen had a conference in New York City where he tried to explain to Hip-Hop artist at that time about going on line. He didn't even use the word going "on line" because that wasn't even a word to describe what the Internet was. It wasn't even called the Internet at that point, it was called BBS boards and things like that. This is what Harry Allen was talking about. Two or three years later, well, not only did he do that, he brought out a magazine called Rap Dot Com and it was at that time the he introduced myself and Chuck D. to the Internet and the rest of you all and explained what this was on. A couple of years later, you all did an album called "Music In Our Message" and on that album was Harry Allen's landmark song which was on limited editions of that album called Harry Allen

Super Mate Its Information Super Highway and phone call to Chuck D. where if you listen to that song every single thing he said in 1993, '94 is true today. He talked about digital distribution, he said that there would be a war going on with some of the major telecommunications companies and record industry execs who would want to reign that in and try to profit off that and that if used correctly it would open the flood gates and allow people to no longer be under the thumb of major record labels. This is in '93 that you all said this. This is propaganda. You all were the first to do an album on line completely from start to finish.

PG: And went on tour with it.

DD: If I remember the history correctly, we also had a situation where there were people who didn't get it that you did this album completely with people from all around the world using digital distribution and the technology and so people were like "I don't like that beat from Australia," and "I don't like this beat from South America," when it was like "Wow, they did this on line, groundbreaking!"

PG: The people in America are slow and late. Everyone around the world got it, you understand what I am saying? But, we are forgetting some milestones now. We are forgetting the fact that production brothers got together. Bring it back now.

DD: I'll let you break it down.

PG: Well, bring it back to the Bomb Squad. Brothers were not basking in their individuality. They came together formed the name called "The Bomb Squad," came up with a Logo, came up with a way of producing together to produce a sound and introduce the whole entire industry to a crew of brothers getting together, producing which is called "The Bomb Squad," that was unheard of!

DD: You know it is interesting, I didn't realize all of you had a hand in it. Flav was telling me that the other day. Can you break that whole thing down, I thought it was just Hank and Keith, but...

PG: It was a lot deeper than that because whether you found the sample, or whether you programmed it and sampled it and put it into the machine, or whether you went to the studio, you had a hand in it. You understand what I am saying? So, it definitely was a collective effort mind and spirit. You didn't necessarily have to be there. You understand what I am saying? If you found a sample and said "Yo, these three samples may not work as far as tempo, but it creates that noise and let's people know the urgency of what is going on with this particular song right here, i.e. "Welcome to the Terror Dome," or "Bring the Noise." Maybe 20, 30 samples and "Welcome to the Terror Dome."

DD: I had the opportunity....

PG: I know about that because we are being sued for it today. (Laughter)

DD: I know, I was going to say that but the brilliance behind it. But one of the things that was interesting was I remember being in the studio for about a week when you all did "Fear For Black Planet," I would never do that again if you all were operating the same way. For people who don't know, I remember driving around the Village with Chuck D. and Eric Sadler and for about two hours that he was looking for a Boris Karloff soundtrack. We finally found it after two hours came back into the studio and then sat there. I know I fell asleep for at least 2 to 3 hours and I woke up and you all still trying to find a part to sample in it. It was meticulous man. I mean, it was crazy!

PG: That is how important that whole concept of creating that particular sound was for us. You had to be meticulous.

DD: You are hearing horns in the background, we are in the Big City, the metropolis of L.A.

PG: Right, see that is typical of what we are talking about because we would have used that sound.

DD: Really?

PG: Of course. We would have used that sound to put that underneath a saxophone, or a drum beat, or a base line to create that mood for that particular song.

DD: So, that was the trick? I just...

PG: Something else now, we're forgetting Professor Griff's role, the Minister of Information. Something unheard of in music. Someone doing research? To research samples and to research snippets and to research material to fuel the songs.

DD: So, those speeches and stuff that was you?

PG: Yeah, of course. My library is extensive man and it's like...

DD: I've heard my voice on a couple of those records (Laughter). I am not going to add to the people to the law suits but I know, I've said "Man is that me in there?"

PG: Right. If you said it and it looked profound we snatched it just to let you all know, but I don't mean to toot my own horn, but that was unheard of in music. The whole idea of the different energies between me, Flava, Chuck. Just Flava's role in and of itself then to fuse that together with the S1W's were doing which is another thing that was unheard of in music. Everybody had dances, no one had soldiers that didn't speak and was ready to take care of business. Then another dynamic, another layer to the whole thing was the whole "Terminator X" thing. These concepts man, were unheard of and these entities were larger than life.

DD: Explain the concept behind "Terminator."

PG: Here is another entity, another layer to Public Enemy that had a mystique about him. Never talked. The whole idea of him being the terminator and then borrowing the whole concept of the Nation of Islam giving brothers who have made it through the FOI an X. And the whole idea of coming up with strategic scratching and cutting at a time where sampling was very, very instrumental and important in Hip-Hop because it served as one of the foundations to create the music, because it was no such thing as a Hip-Hop record.

DD: Let's get this straight, we are going back into '86 and '87 that you all are coming up with these concepts?

PG: No, we are going a little bit further back than that because the concept had to be understood, introduced, understood and developed.

DD: So how far back does Public Enemy go then? We were introduced to you all in '87, but then I have the record "Spectrum City" that goes back ever further, so can you talk about those early beginnings?

90

PG: Naw, you are talking about Professor Griff and Hank Shockley, long before Chuck D. came into the picture.

DD: Really? O.K.

PG: DJ Griff, and Hank Shockley, and Keith Shockley, and Jerry Jay then after that came the Chuck D.

DD: What years are we talking?

PG: I'm about to tell my age right now, but it's alright. You're talking when I was 18, 1978, 1977.

DD: You guys go back to the '70's, so pioneers for real?

PG: I was in bands before Public Enemy so, I was already into music and it wasn't until later on that Chuck D. came along and I hope he don't mind me saying this, but, he'll tell you, he use to listen, be in the audience and listen to D.J. Griff. This is regal man. So, when people write our history, and I'm glad we are talking about this, because when you read the history of Public Enemy you don't read this. This is why you are so valuable. I don't mean to toot your horn, but this is why this medium right now is so valuable because we can get the real. I was DJing long before Chuck was that voice.

DD: And this is being said in the spirit of accuracy, not a spirit of dis-ing.

PG: Right. Definitely not a spirit of dis-ing

DD: **Someone would pick that up like, "Oh, you hate them!"**

PG: No, no, definitely love Chuck, Flava and the whole crew. Everybody served their particular purpose and their role and I think we are good at it.

DD: Now this is important because I was talking with the S1W's to get some of that history. Let's do this, let's take a break because I want to come back and talk about this other important concept and we will be right back.

DD: We're back here, Davey D. hanging out with you this afternoon. We have been talking to Professor Griff, you know celebrating the 20th anniversary of Public Enemy, legendary Hip-Hop groups. One of the greatest music groups of all time and going back to the very, very beginnings and before we went Griff was talking about being Professor Griff and being with Hank Shockley, two of the cornerstones of the infamous "Bomb Squad" that really architect the sound of P.E. and you all are going back to '77 being in a band and all that. One of the things I want to get into the roles of the S1W's. I was talking with Flav the other night and he was saying that he played 14 instruments, you guys were in a band, so can you talk about the whole importance of that instrumentation because other than "Full Force" and maybe one or two other groups (in stet sonic) you didn't have a lot of East coast groups playing instruments as you did on the West coast where you have everybody was a band. When we coming up we didn't have bands in our high school. But then again you were outside of New York and didn't have the budget cuts.

PG: No, we didn't. We were in plush Long Island, green grass, sunny skies you know and people think right now to this day that Public Enemy is from Long Island? But, a lot of people from around the world just don't know, have never been to Long Island so they wouldn't know, but bringing it back to the subject, if you went to the studio back in the days, late '70's and you didn't know how to play an instrument, sing or do something, what are you doing there? You just didn't hang out. You understand what I am saying? So you had to know how to do something, you just didn't hang out, with that said, what are you doing here? Now a day you get one artist, one producer, one DJ at a studio but 30 dudes are there. For what? You understand what I am saying? We need to understand this concept. Back then, you had to know how to do something, today, it's just not like that. So, in taking those talents, respect for the studio, that respect for your craft, that time that you put into it and bringing it to the forefront and bringing it to the studio now that there is sampling machines, it's like, "What am I going to do with these last 10, 15 years I spent perfecting my craft?" So we said, "Why not sample the musician as opposed to sampling the record? So, we did both and this added to the whole creation of the sound."

DD: So, now when you all did this, Flav said he was part of the "Bomb Squad" to. Everybody came in there and chipped in and played a lick or something.

PG: Well, Chuck was in the studio in Hank Shockley's basement. We came up with some corny songs that we were doing in the basement and we pressed it to acetate. Literally man, with drums and banging on the pipes and that kind of thing. This is real man.

DD: Are there any outtakes that would be really embarrassing that you all were trying to work out. I mean you don't have to let us hear them but tell us some of the concepts that you all were playing around with.

PG: Not necessarily embarrassing, but very kind of interesting. "Check Out the Radio" from Chucky D. We need to dig up that record.

DD: I have that.   We are going to play that, "Spectrum City." Let's take a break. We'll be right back. I got that one. So, here we go, so Chuck D. was Chucky D.?

PG: Chucky D, which he would admit himself, was corny, so I think that is when the Hank Shockley/Griff connection came back into fruition.   So what happened to the dude, yada, yada, ya, whoop de whoop, and whatever. Oh ok, we need to bring him back. A part of this Public Enemy thing, but I was doing something totally different as far as music is concerned.   By that time, the ungodly Disco music was playing out and sadly enough we may not want to admit it and you may not want to admit, Disco played a pivot part in bringing to birth, Hip-Hop.

DD: Because it was a rejection. A lot of people don't understand that Disco was being rejected and out of the hatred for Disco, it left a void which gave birth to Funk/Hip-Hop.

PG: Now, let's not disrespect Disco all together because what records did we have to go back to get them free.

DD: What I am talking about is there was a formula in Disco because there were two strands that came out of the Disco era.   One strand went on and kept the Gospel, soulful vocals, the driving baselines and it had a DJ culture attached to it, had the pounding and it did what Hip-Hop did, it remade a lot of classic records.   With the skill sets and resource that people have, today, we know that music as House Music coming out in the late '70's, from a New York transplant into Chicago, Frankie Knuckles.

PG: .....birth to what?

DD: House gave birth to a lot of things.

93

PG: Techno, and that kind of thing, Electronica, and a lot of smaller genres of music.

DD: And the other strand was of course, Hip-Hop.

PG: Right, exactly. So now, Hip-Hop came to birth. You have musicians that have experienced the Funk era that went through the Disco era and was now experimenting with sampling machines and formulating this thing called Hip-Hop. Now we can roll the pages back and look at "Full Force," "Soul Sonic Force," "Africa Bambaataa" and the outlandish clothes and the gear.

DD: Flashing all that. That was all out of the Funk era.

PG: That's the Funk era. We borrowed from the Funk era. We borrowed from....

DD: Did you all have leather pants? Did you all wear leather pants?

PG: You are out of your mind. (Laughter)

DD: But I've looked at those album covers, Bam, Flash, and everybody did wear the leather pants. Now, when I talked to Flash and they said they wore the leather pants cause that was the performance gear at that time.

PG: Exactly, that is because there was no such thing as Hip-Hop gear. We've got to keep in mind these are new concepts. A Hip-Hop record, hip-hop gear, hip-hop lingo and that kind of thing. There was no such thing as that. It was something we just did. It was organic. You understand what I am saying? So, it was formulating then so someone had to stop it and put a structure to it. Then came Bambaattaa who put the structure to it and said this is the foundation of it. This is what it is about and we followed it that is why he is the Godfather of Hip-Hop.

PG: That's real talk right there. We have been talking to Professor Griff of Public Enemy. We talked about some of these landmark concepts and I was going through time on the technology tip, but you stopped me and said the milestones. Let's talk about the very important milestones of the S1W's. I talked with Brother James and he gave a history and he was like, you know, obviously you are the master sensei when it comes to this martial arts thing. Maybe you can talk about that whole thing. About you all securing, holding down, keeping off the gangs, the whole importance of bringing the type of discipline that you all did with the martial arts and the S1W's and how that manifest itself throughout the legacy of Public Enemy.

PG: Once again, we are talking about brothers and let's get that other thing straight first. I am not the master of Pop, Diesel, and Public Enemy. One of the S1W's was one of my teachers. So, we kind of kept it all in. I was taught by him.

DD: He taught you?

PG: He taught me.

DD: Man, everybody talks about you taught them.

PG: No, no no, no Pop taught me. I was a student of Pop and surprisingly enough there were 2 or 3 women I was under who taught me. So I got my instructions from women in martial arts and from Pop.

DD: Where there any women in S1W?

PG: Of course, Sister Aisha, Sister Simone. There was a lot of women who were female S1W's.

DD: OK got it. I just don't remember seeing them there.

PG: They were there but the discipline it takes to acquire a first and second and third degree black belt oh it takes a lot of discipline and time. That also went into the Public Enemy formula. We have got to stop thinking so surface that Public Enemy is Chuck and Flav and they're just rappers. This thing has multi-layers to it. If you dig, you will find out that you have to dig deeper.

DD: So let's talk about the S1W's and the concept and how this all played out. When I was talking with Brother James, I was talking about the important connection between Hip-Hop and martial arts.

PG: Well, Drew and Mike being my students who are now the sound man and road manager for Public Enemy and that is even deep because they have a long history of music. Their father has been playing music up in the church ever since I can remember and had a kind of Deacon, kind of aide relationship with my people in the church, Reverend Mackey's church, Mount Sinai Baptist Church. But their father got a long history of playing. So, all these entities are coming together. Now, I don't live there, I grew up right

95

across the street from Pop, so we always had that connection and then being introduced and meeting Brother James and Little James, Big James, Brother Roger, Crunch.

DD: I forgot about Crunch. Man, you went back into time. I forgot....

PG: So there is a long history of every 6 degrees in separation somebody knowing somebody who knows somebody creating this very, very foundation of what Public Enemy stands on today. There has been a long history of S1W's.

DD: Now the S1W's was your own protection. Can you talk about that?

PG: Well, we were once Unity Force. An organization that I had put together with James, Roger, the other James, Pop came a little bit later on, Mike was introduced to it. Drew was there and what we were doing was setting up study groups for brothers coming out of jail and setting up study groups in the community. We were setting up martial arts classes, free! We weren't getting paid for this. This was community work which is another thing we introduced to the Public Enemy thing that leads us into going into prisons and doing community work. So the whole idea of Public Enemy probably gave birth in our subconscious mind a long time ago. The physical Pubic Enemy thing came to birth when the actual public seen it, but we were already groomed for this.

DD: Which is why when you did come into fruition, the public knew you through records. You all seem to be able to hit the ground running in terms of being mature, and...

PG: Knowing how to do community work. We were already groomed for it. And you know Brother Dwayne and Ben Ransom and Brother Jacob who actually sacrificed their time, losing their jobs and that kind of thing to establish the Public Enemy presence on the road. They cannot be forgotten.

DD: Let me ask you this; you know with so much information and so much knowledge how much pressure was there and could you realistically put all these concepts and ideas with the depth, with the urgency and the importance on record. Could you really capture what you all were experiencing out on the community, on vinyl, and to what advantage did these records have for you and to what disadvantage did it have to you.

PG: It wasn't until Chuck came up with the brilliant idea of buying cameras and saying "Look man, we are going to film our own stuff because you are not going to understand the magnitude of what Public Enemy is about just listening to a song."

DD: And so another first, a lot of rappers started doing straight to video, and straight to DVD thing, if you are old enough you will probably have copies of the '80's of PETV. This was a concept way before Master P and a lot of P, and no disrespect, you all were pioneers in that. I remember people looked at you all crazy like "What you'll doing?"

PG: And we get no credit for it.

DD: I have that original video. PETV when you all were doing the news.

PG: Exactly, and people just don't understand that. People say "Well you all were ahead of your time, now is the time." But if we gave birth to you, don't you think you should come around and say "Okay, these are the brothers that kicked down the door. Let me hook back up with these brothers so we can set this thing straight, so that next generation that comes won't introduce pornography and marry it on the Hip-Hop, won't introduce the criminal element and marry it on the Hip-Hop, won't introduce the bourgeoisie element or the Uncle Tom scenario into Hip-Hop. We need to guard that. Someone needs to protect the culture."

DD: You know it is interesting that when you all were coming up with these concepts, it was parallel to another group of people who had concepts that were being born the same time, the Black Watch movement which eventually gave birth to X-Clan and then of course, KRS1 was foundering then figuring things out, but I don't think you were as attached to movements as much. I mean Bambaattaa and those guys would have probably been more attached to movements and I think they got neutralized, unfortunately, by '86 in terms of their influence.

PG: Brother that is another first now. Now you have movements in Hip-Hop creating –I'm not saying that we created the whole concept of a crew-because there was "Crash Crew" and all the other crews, Funky Four plus One More, Traitorous Three and a whole bunch of crews. But I am saying crews that had an agenda and created movement. You can't call it a movement unless you are moving the masses of people. Whether you are moving their spirit, or their minds or their bodies. You understand what I am saying? That is another first. Because now we are setting up strategic government offices and people had to head those offices. You understand what I am saying? Because when you speak outside the context of a song and CD, what are you going to talk about? What kind of gear you got on? How many pairs of sneakers you got? Your watch? No. This is real talk to move real people about real issues and this is what we are suffering with today. There is not enough of us heading these offices to speak to certain issues.

DD: Right, I hear that.

PG: One of the purposes that the S1W's serve. We are here to say that we are first world people, not third world people and we stuck to that and we drove it home that we are first world people doing two things; raising the collective conscious and collective self-esteem of our people. Pricking the conscious of those who want to relegate us to niggerdom, borrowed that from Cat Williams. Do you understand what I am saying? We fought this to turn around in 2007 from 1987 to have brothers and sisters call themselves niggers.

DD: We are back here celebrating the 20th anniversary of Public Enemy. You know one of the under talked about collaborations with P.E. and I never understood why it didn't go to the next level was when P.E. hooked up with a woman named Lisa Williamson who we got to know as Sista Soulja. The landmark song "We Are At War," "Buck Walden." What was it like to have that collaboration, to have that female energy, and why didn't we see it go to the next level especially when she put out her album. If you get the "360 Degrees of Power" album now, it was definitely ahead of its time as well.

PG: I think the Professor Griff controversy at that time over shadowed a lot of things that were very monumental and instrumental that Public Enemy was saying and doing at the time. If you can remember, I wasn't there on the scene when those things were going down, it was just kind of one of those things that was put out there and because the Professor Griff thing was going on, there was not enough attention focused on the beautiful artistry and energy of that sister and what she bought to Public Enemy. People viewed it as she was trying to replace Professor Griff and that wasn't the case. It was just that next level.

DD: She was already an activist doing big things. I remember when she was coming to the new music seminars, Lisa Williams was throwing down and she was known all through Rutgers University, so she was a heavy weight herself.

PG: Yes, in her own right. She didn't necessarily need Public Enemy. I think in that situation to take the attention off what was going down with me, I think Public Enemy made a strategic move and pulled her in. And I think it was very strategic because we didn't necessarily make songs that appealed to women. The average woman and it was a very beautiful thing which she brought in the spirit she brought. I can't honestly say women took notice even after then, but I think it gave birth to the conscious female rapper sort of speaking. Because, let's think now and I am challenging you and myself at this time, name the female rappers at that time that was conscious?

DD: Now, let's see. You had Queen Latifah was coming out around that time...

PG: Which I use to road manage.

DD: I didn't know that.

PG: Of course. Definitely

DD: You use to road manage.

PG: Yes! Me and Shakim. I kind of had him under my wing, showing him the ropes and, I use to manage Queen Latifah.

DD: Ok. I didn't know that. Miss Dana Owens. I remember when she blew up the spot at the New Music seminars, two pony tails and some overalls. The man didn't know why her records weren't on the radio. Had people shook, okay, but then you had the poetess out here. When she came out, her album was kind of conscious and like Sista Soulja, she did have poetry, spoken word on hers "Simply Poetry." And then you know the conscious daughters, they came a few years later. But you know, Salt 'N Peppa...

PG: *psssstt*....conscious female rappers.

DD: Even though they had good messages.

PG: Exactly, because we don't understand the levels of consciousness, we are not going to get deep, but if there is different levels of consciousness, you might hear something in this song that elevated your consciousness whatever level you are on. So it didn't have to be the super, super, super deeds "Oh, man they are talking about the government, they are raising my consciousness." No, it could have been something that talked about food, talked about your self-esteem, talked about you being a good mother or father. In raising your awareness, none the less it was still consciousness on a certain degree.

DD: You had Body and Soul. Queen Nefertiti.

PG: Whom I managed also.

DD: Queen Nefertiti?

PG: She is on my earlier stuff. I titled her album "Life: Living in Fear of Extinction."

DD: I didn't realize that and then of course we had the two MC Lyte, of course was just really starting to flow, and then we had the Hardcore Sisters and X-Clan, Queen Mother Rage and Isis.

PG: Right, none the less at that time and prior to that, I forget her name and she is going to kill me, we had the Roxanne Chantes, we had the real Roxanne, we had other females that were there. Miss Melody brought a certain level of energy to the table. There were other woman that were there we didn't perceive them as being conscious female artist though, which is the sad part about it, because our definition of consciousness was given to us, which is sad, rather than us defining it for ourselves.

Breakdown FM Part 2

The History of Public Enemy August 21, 2007
Davey D- Moderator (DD)
Professor Griff- Guest Speaker (PG)

DD: Davey D. hanging out with you this afternoon. We have moved our conversation from Los Angeles to San Francisco continuing our discussion with Professor Griff celebrating the 20th anniversary of Public Enemy. In the background you hear the Wu-Tang Gang doing their thing but we are chopping it up. You know, you have given us rich history of Public Enemy and talking about the legacy and we were walking up through time and where we left off you were beginning to the challenging years that took place when you guys had, if the word "falling out" is the word, then I want you to talk about how you all were able to overcome that period. And what even led up to it with the remarks you were attributed to, and how that caused a fall-out and for a second put a stop or slowed up the momentum of one of the most impactful groups in music ever.

PG: To recap that whole thing would be painful, number one, then very lengthy number two, I think the thing that led up to was the fact from the out start, not even Davey D. knew it was only suppose to be a 2 year program.

DD: Public Enemy was.

PG: That's right. Two years, that is it. So, if we start at the end of '86, '87, by into '88, '89 was suppose to be a wrap.

DD: Was there plans to do anything afterwards?

PG: No, there wasn't. Shock said himself, "We will either be dead, or, we would be in the hospital or in jail. So, we were supposed to get in for two years, make our mark and get out.

DD: So, you all were surprised to see it continue on like this?

PG: I don't think that was my particular thinking at that time. My particular thinking at that time was the fact that "We're out!" This is not something we are going to prolong and stay in. So, anything that was said and done be it against the Clan, of

101

Zionism, or Israeli occupation, or Iran, or America, whoever else, is like, did it make a difference? Come battle on the political, intellectual front. You understand what I am saying? So, I never knew what took place back then in '89 would even take place. You know, there was a lot of talk about a whole bunch of things like it is now on the tour bus, behind stage, in the dressing room, at home, in the studio you never think that stuff is going to get out and end up on somebody's front page. Now, if we were to "air someone's laundry" so to speak, let's just say yours. Something you and your closest friends talk about would you want 80% of that stuff put out?

DD: Right.

PG: The things that is supposed to be kept within the circle here was suppose to have been kept in the circle. Since there was information that was supposed to be disseminated by James Bomb, one of the S1W's it was cool to hand out the pamphlets, Dr. Frances Cress-Welsings pamphlet, information we were putting out on the Black Panther Party, the flyers that we would put out, the things that we would talk about in the prisons and the hospitals and that kind of thing. For me, to think that all of these things would lead to my brothers,- who I grew up with since four and five years old-kicking me out of the group, oh man, that was unheard of dude.

DD: And this was the group you were the founding member?

PG: Yes! As though this was like a job, you know, like you were suspended. How do you suspend somebody from a rock group? So I said on VH1 "Niggas can get shot for sh_t like that man! Cause now, this is some other sh_t." You understand what I am saying? I didn't understand where that was coming from.

DD: Well, obviously there was a lot of outside forces that wanted to see that happen and I remember people were talking about for a while that there was concern that Public Enemy needed to be reined in. That the political messages that were being put out and they were unbridled and especially, if it came to you, that there was no control over Griff, there was no way to pre-approve your remarks before they came out and keeping in mind there hadn't been a political group in that era that was like a public enemy.

PG: Real quick. That is not true. There was a way. No one took the time to sit down and make the strategy.

DD: No, I'm talking about outside forces. People that have nothing to do with Public Enemy.

PG: Outside forces spoke to Chuck's feeling and thinking at that time and I think he followed suit. Anyone could have come in there, I am a military strategist. Anyone could have come to me and said "Yo, we might not want to do that. Let's say it this way, let's do it that way." Cool, if that is the strategy. But, no one said anything about a strategy, we were out. Now, all of a sudden you want to stay in and do what? Oh dude, we have got to do some damage control, but no one wanted to do damage control. F_ck the nigga, kick him nigga out....as though I'm worthless. That's sad.

DD: I remember when I talked to you, obviously, it was painful for you I remember when I saw that I felt that when I talked to you and it was also very painful for a lot of people that were fans of Public Enemy because up to this point in a lot of ways P.E. represented our manhood so to speak. You were the blocks, you were the fist of fury that were holding people at bay and to see that crack in the armor was something that I just remember people was like "Aw man, I can't believe this!" And it also seemed that there was potential for a lot of things to happen because there were people definitely siding with Griff, there were people that were definitely siding with Chuck's point of view. You know what I mean? You could see how things could unfold into something else. I bring this up to ask and to share with all listeners the steps you all were able to take to repair that. To not allow it to get out of control and I think one of the things I knew just from being around you all was that I was offered a lot of money shortly after you had come to our radio station and people heard you on the air when you had joined up with Luke's Records...

PG: No, no, go back. No joining up.

DD: No, I'm saying when you were signed.

PG: That was Chuck's doing.

DD: I don't know. Let's come back to that. But what I was getting at was that there were magazines that were offering lots and lots of money to get this expose, "Griff vs. Chuck." There was a lot of folks and fortunately I think, most of the journalist that were approached either one, didn't have the information or two, was just like "I'm just not doing it." I know I turned it down and I think anyone close to you turned it down but the fact is that was something people were gunning for and in retrospect it was very interesting to see that there was a lot riding on seeing dissention in that group because the dissention in the group was going to be something that could potentially lead to dissention over ideology, or perceived ideology for followers, fan and just the community in general.

PG: Wow that is a lot in a question.

DD: It was more of a statement.

PG: The whole language of me joining with Luke

DD: I might have mis-quote that, so we can clear that up.

PG: It was kind of disturbing. That disturbs me because it was Chuck who went down and got me the deal with Luke. I wasn't a rapper. I was the Minister of Information, I was no M.C. So what am I doing signing a contract with Luke to make some records? I wasn't making records. I ain't think about making records. You understand what I am saying? Each one of us has a special relationship with our slave master's children. Your relationship with them is your relationship with them you understand what I am saying? But, this is where I feel I erred, so to speak. I took the mature route and didn't make this records, didn't gun for them, didn't kill them, burn down their house all the things I could of done, I didn't do that. We met with the minister, he said Chuck's the leader, let him lead. If he wants you out of the group that is what you have to accept. I accepted that and I pushed on. I didn't ask for no deal, I didn't ask for no money for nothing. Chuck went to Def Jam and had Def Jam pay me for some stuff they hadn't paid me for. Chuck went back to the group and said "Griff is going to be alright." He got a little bit of chump change. I'm not in it for the money, never was. Didn't want any money from anyone. I wanted to raise the consciousness of our people, but trying times like that Chuck, Griff and everyone in situation better men.   And hopefully people like you that was on the periphery of it look in and said ok.   I still know those brothers, I am still cool with them you understand, and it's nice to see them getting along.   But it was a very trying time because I got poisoned.   I had to move my children out of school.   I had to do a whole bunch of things while those dudes was eating well.   I was starving, they was eating.   I was kicked to the curb to die and that kind of stuff is painful man.

DD: You know, when we see so many groups broken up and they've gone through their differences and this being a very glaring example of that, how were you able to repair that? How can people learn from that?   You know, 20 years you all have been together, and this, obviously, from the outside looking in seemed to probably be the most difficult one. Considering that people kill each other over the smallest things...like you said, people might have understood if anything crazy went out of....   But people go to war over slights, you know, "I don't like what he said." "I don't like what he looked like."   How did you all repair that?   How did you all reconcile some of that?

PG: I think all of us had to grow up and accept our responsibility in creating the atmosphere that a young, revolutionary like Professor Griff will make the kind of remarks that he made. Not to repeat the remarks and get into that, but some people that came to me studied the remarks and put them under the microscope and found the remarks to be very, very accurate.   Call me what you want to call me but it is not about Griff.   If I made a statement, put the statement under the microscope.   Don't attack me and kill the messenger. "Okay, what did he say?" Without taking it out of context, say what did he say, put it under the microscope.   Each one of us had to do that and grow up and accept the fact that timing was bad, the spirit in which you delivered it, who you delivered it to, very, very bad Griff.   I had to learn from that and suffer the consequences. Do you understand what I am saying?   So we learned valuable lessons in war strategy, keeping things in its proper context, who we allow and give interviews to. That is a science in and of itself. Cause I have learned, you know I have learned that the best of them that give interviews, don't take interviews from anybody.

DD: I've seen you turn down interviews with people.

PG: I have turned down 3 today! I just said, "No thank you" I've been to interviews where they literally want to attack me and bring the same Jewish controversy back up and I'm like "No thank you." Jewish people, all they wanted was an apology, out in the open, up front in which Chuck gave them. Which I was not giving anybody. Look, this is my position, let's talk. We could talk. We could sit down and talk about my position and if I feel I owe someone an apology, I'll apologize because I am man enough to do that. What I apologized for was the spirit and manner in which I presented some stuff I thought was factual information, you know what I am saying? That is what I have to accept. Now, politically, if you don't think it is factual, then come debate me, without the anger and try to take my life. Plain and simple, so have I lost Jewish friends that I was friends with back...no, because they are mature enough to understand it. Were young Jews that was coming up angry at Professor Griff? Yes. Did I take my time to go to Holocaust museums and sit down with Jewish people creating programs like "Bridging the Gap?" Yes. Did I go through some 12 step program that Chuck was talking about? Hell no! I wasn't doing nothing like that. I am a realist man and I speak with passion and I speak from the heart. A lot of good friends I have out there, that are White, Black, Jew and Gentile, you understand what I am saying? And we talk about a wide variety of things. If I was to put some of those things on the air right now, you would be surprised. But those are things are made not to be put on the air like that and they put it on the front page of someone's newspaper. But no one questions David Mill's intent.

DD: You know it is an interesting thing being a journalist. We have had these debates with other journalist especially when we are in the Hip-Hop arena because of the nature of this culture, there is a thin line we run as being friends and being professionals. For example, me being around you guys, I see off-color moments, I see on-color moments. But I don't put the on-color moments

PG: Now you wouldn't put no off-color moments on.

DD: I don't even put the on-color moments on. It's a thing if I know that I am with you as a journalist, then I am there as a journalist, and we have conversation like we're interviewing now. But if I was in the room and we are having conversation like we were before that is Dave the friend, that has nothing to do with anybody knowing that I don't share conversations I have with my friends in a public space and I shouldn't do the same there. And I think like you said, and one thing I have learned over the years is that when you have friends that are in powerful positions, meaning people look up to them, there is a lot that gets weighed. I found this out the hard way with Chuck when we had an off-color, I wouldn't say off-color, just a private conversation about his feelings about Tupac when he passed. Chuck had these 18 reasons he was just rattling off as we are talking like "Man I don't think he is really dead cause a, b, c, and d. It sounded fascinating at the time. I put it out on the Internet not thinking that Chuck my friend is Chuck D. of Public Enemy. Man when that went out, the rumors still persist today. You know, we were on Nightline, they kept bringing up, you know what I 'm saying and it became a whole bigger thing than life, but then we learned and I learned I've got to remember that me seeing Griff is Davey D. hanging out and me seeing Griff as the Minister of Information for Public Enemy is going to be very different once it goes out to the people and so, we've got be very clear and as you said, almost strategic.

PG: Right and that is very wise and that is very intelligent and I am going to be honest with you. If I had to roll the time back and do it all over again, of course, I would have done it different. A lot of times when you say things, words have a frequency to them. Words have vibration to them man, and you don't know what you are saying and how it is going to hit people when, you know what I am saying? That I definitely had to learn. We have to understand something there was circumstances surrounding that period.

DD: People were gunning for you.

PG: I was the road manager, having to deal with Flava, Minister of Information, leader of the S1W's, all of these roles.

DD: And a young man trying to figure out the business.

PG: A young man trying to figure out the business and still try to make ends meet and still growing up frustrated and angry without a father. Do you understand what I am saying? So, all of these things, I'm not making excuses, I don't want people to get me wrong, do you understand what I am saying, but that is the real.

DD: Well, I think the other interesting aspect to that is that I know when I made a decision not to speak on what I knew, there were attacks that came, and I am sure, not just with me, but other journalist, from fellow journalist who insisted that the public had a right to know. I thought that was a very interesting switch. Like the public has a right to know and there were some that bought into it. Fortunately, I had been working at major radio stations and other places where I got to see that the public that the type of decision making I made was something that was routinely practiced. Meaning, there are very famous singers, for example, that come to the station that are gay but they are heartthrobs to the industry. They are heartthrobs to their fans, or they are on drugs and the industry keeps it quiet. There have been very famous artist that we witnessed at our Summer Jam concerts smack their girlfriends, punch out their wives, very famous that the morning show is told not to talk about that on the air. I just say that because the public doesn't have a right to know and as I said, these off-color moments don't need to be shared with the public. Artist got to be allowed to be artist, and it's not a cool thing, but we are not going to participate in that. So, it is very interesting to see that those things are routinely practiced. That there are those artist that cross these lines where all kinds of seasoned journalist turn the other way, but when it came to Public Enemy, then they wanted it to be open. They wanted the whole book to be out there, the public had the right to know. But the public doesn't have the right to know about who is singing love songs, but they are not into women; which famous artist is beating their wife back stage, being paid a hundred thousand dollars sitting up there and getting all types of accolades, but nobody wants to say it. Who is bringing a gun to the station, and then showing up on trial? You understand what I am saying? Those are the types of double standards that routinely existed.

PG: Right and I see it all the time. That is what I tell people. I don't tell my story, I don't do lectures and that sort of thing and speak from a bumper sticker perspective. I live this. You and I can write a book on just what we have seen today.

DD: A lot of stuff that we've seen.

PG: You know what I am saying? I wouldn't air that stuff man, it's like, what I try to do is learn and had to learn discernment, I had to learn, and you know a lot of times you just have to shut up and don't speak. Let things take a pass, and say, "Ok, I m going to deal with that later," i.e. the Flava roast, i.e. Flava of Love 1, 2 and now 3 coming. Some things you just have to say, "Okay, I'm going to let it ride and I'm going to see how to deal with that and in my maturity I know how to deal with that."

DD: Now, that's real talk. Now how do people learn from that? What's a couple of steps that people need to learn so that we don't act on the emotion and suddenly, because of something we don't like...

PG: I don't think that we should think that there is the 'boogey-man' theory, I call it. There is always the boogey-man hiding under the bed, or in the closet. The guy behind the curtain is actually controlling things and we shouldn't buy into that particular theory, you understand what I am saying? I think we ought to stand up as real men and deal with issues, real issues, like real men. Plain and simple. There was a time you and I use to bump heads on certain issues in reference to Chuck, understand what I am saying? But, I think, you and I kept in contact, kept a level of respect. I wasn't doing nothing for you, I wasn't trying to kill you , or the hell with Davey D. yada, yada, yada, naw, to the point where maybe down the road we could kind of reunite and do some things together so that people that are coming up look at that part of history and learn from it. So, some valuable lessons I got out of it I had to learn discernment, I had to learn, look, a lot of times you have to be careful who you are speaking to and what you are saying. These are things people don't look at once again. Who is looking at what reward did David Mills get? He is in Hollywood now, famous writer, New York Undercover and some other television shows he writes for, see we don't look at these things. Did David Mills do it again, look at Sista Souljah. We don't look at these things. So, is he an agent and how we deal with that? Are you following me?

DD: No, I definitely hear that. I found that there were a lot of people that were rewarded and some people actually took the bacon when they gave bad reviews to Public Enemy. There were three columnists, I remember the first black columnist to really gun for the group, not because of a bad record but to gun for you all personally which was unheard of at that time. One of them, Torre from Rolling Stone was bragging, you know like "My review ended the career of Public Enemy." This is an e-mail he sent me five years ago, so it's like, wow, these are the things people get off on. So, black or white, every brother is not a brother and some people are in it for the money on both sides of the track. Not just on the rap tip, but sometimes on the journalism tip as well.

PG: Right. You are absolutely right man and I just hope that people learn valuable lessons cause I did. This is the 20th year of Public Enemy and we are trying to do monumental things in our own right and then hopefully something that we say or do may affect you. You may not agree with everything we say, hell, I don't and I am in the d_mn group! I don't agree with everything so, but, I am rolling with the punches and I am here to make positive contributions.

DD: Let me ask you, let's go back to you said earlier you were not a rapper and if you are just tuning in, we are talking to Professor Griff, 20th anniversary of Public Enemy. He has given us a lot of insight, lot of history people didn't know and this is definitely eye opening. But let's talk about when you were Professor Griff and the Last Asiatic Disciples. So you were not a rapper, but you went off and did that and what was that whole experience like with the Last Asiatic Disciples?

PG: See, but we are going right back to the controversy. My life was being threatened then.

DD: Really, I didn't know that.

PG: Shot at, the whole bit. Then Chuck got me a deal with Luke. I'm like, "Okay, what do I do with that?" So I went out and found brothers that could rap, because I couldn't! Put together the Last Asiatic Disciples and if you go back to the album, I maybe rapped on one or two songs, but I was doing some poetry stuff or something. I knew how to put music together from being around the Bomb Squad, but other than that man I wasn't no rapper. I wasn't checking for that.

DD: I hear that. But, you did do some spoken word on another album though?

PG: Yes I did the song, "Love Your Enemy" dedicated to Public Enemy. I was letting them know on the album, it ain't no beef because you definitely don't want me to take it there. You understand what I am saying? Naw, we wouldn't be here today dude, for real.

DD: Doing the spoken word then we seen you morph into doing the 7th Octaves, the rock and roll version of that. What's the relationship with music per say, if you are not a rapper, do you like to do the spoken word, do you like to express yourself on stage? How do we see you?

PG: The conversation we had in L.A., the first part of this conversation, I was already in a band before Public Enemy. I was already a DJ. Chuck was already in the audience when I was DJ-ing. Chuck will tell you for himself, "Griff was my first DJ I ever experienced getting down." So I was always into music. This is just another phase and aspect, that's all. I've been on stage before. I was on Eddie Murphy's first tour, Lord Have Murphy.

DD: Really? I didn't know that.

PG: I was on there with Kyle Jason.

DD: Oh man, you guys really, really do go back.

PG: I was his road manager, so I got history. You understand what I am saying? So all this is nothing new to me man, absolutely nothing new to me at all. So, I think that's why Hank and Chuck made a wise decision, we need to get that brother.

DD: Kyle Jason?

PG: No, me. To do the road managing thing and the S1W thing and the whatever when we put the Public Enemy thing together. I was already seasoned in everybody you see here in Public Enemy I kind of brought to the fold.

DD: That is rich history there. We are going to let people marinate on that and we are going to take a break. I want to find out where things are in 2007. We are back here talking to Professor Griff, walking down memory lane as we are celebrating the 20th anniversary of Public Enemy. How do you feel the group is perceived today with respect to a very politicized atmosphere, war, Bush, six years stolen election, Katrina, all these different things at the same time. There has been a concern expressed by many, especially that came out of our generation that a lot of the artist aren't directly addressing this, at least not the ones that have the most stage presence in terms of being on video and radio everyday and we see this concern that there is a lack of leadership, you know, the same leaders we had 30 years ago are still those leaders, and we're asking where is the next crop and what is going to be the next step. How do you see that especially in relationship to Public Enemy?

PG: Wow that is a deep question. I really admire you for just having the testosterone for putting that together man, because that was critical. Where do I start? It's like the whole idea of grooming other governments, and other people, other cultures, other nationalities, grooming leaders to lead their people is a concept that we as a people need to take hold of. We were talking earlier and we were saying there is not even a monument for us to go visit and walk around the monument and give honor and praise to Malcolm X. We have one for Dr. King, but there are so many of us that are dead and gone that we just forget about them. Other people don't operate that way. They erect statues and libraries full of information, foundations and that kind of thing to keep that persons memory alive. The political climate and I am going to sum this up because I have to get back out here. The political climate that surrounds Public Enemy today is just as it was 20 years ago. You say the same leaders are around, and they are around today doing what though? If the climate is the same and worse, what are we doing different? What is the clinical definition of insane, '...doing the same thing over and over and over and expecting a different result,' and we are doing the same thing over, expecting something or someone to change our reality.

DD: Now people might say well Public Enemy are leaders too. So, has there been a different kind of approach that you bring to the game, knowing you literally walk in both worlds?

PG: We've talked about that earlier with what we are doing as far as the 8 or 9 "firsts" we talked about in LA. The whole idea of Flava being the greatest hype man ever in the history of hip-hop is something in and of itself because now you watch young people's hype men and, you understand what I am saying, and it's just not there, they are just not cutting it. You lend to what the lead rapper is doing. The whole idea of crews getting together as production teams was unheard back then, you following me? The whole idea of my office, the minister of information, is unheard of in hip-hop. Researching the material that you put in your songs which I think something is needed today from this madness you hear in these lyrics. So, I'm thinking in the first, I think we are leading the way in some of these things. Now, we are not leading the way in the whole political thing, maybe, that is not our area. If we are not leading the way in journalism, maybe that is your area. We are fighting the battles were we can fight them, you understand what I am saying? I think everybody should just do their job where they are at. I'm not going to try to go make donuts man, I don't know how to make donuts. You understand what I am saying? I know how to do what I do, that's to disseminate information. I am a researcher.

DD: That's real talk there. Sometimes we might put too much of an expectation.

PGL: Exactly.

DD: You know, you sing the song, you gave the information, why can't you just put together the entire solution and solve the problem, while we sit back?

PG: I do a three hour lecture and people expect me to have all the solutions. No, I'm giving you this information so you can take it and run with it, are you following me?

DD: Yes.

PG: Okay.

DD: Let me ask you this, 2008, electoral politics is on the table, anybody resonating, anybody hitting the mark with issues that you think need to be spoken about? Are all of them short of the mark and if so, which way should we be going or at least considering? Now I am asking you to put on your Minister of Information hat.

PG: To the people that are listening to the sound of my voice, I'm going to call out some names, however it resonates when the vibratory frequency hits you wherever it hits you, then you can decide and choose for yourself alright? Fred Hampton Jr., the POCC, the New Black Panther Party, The Nation of Islam, all of those street organizations, regardless of the name or regardless of the color. All of those organizations that are fighting for the liberation of our people. I don't care if you are in America, or another country, all of those like-minded people that can support revolutionary causes that is who I am shooting for, that is the spirit I'm going for. Chuck D. teaches all the time that this two party system is not going to cut it man. I stopped voting a long time ago, because the vote is a scam! You understand what I am saying? Like you said earlier, they select the President.

DD: But what about our local elections where you live in local communities...

PG: Can I speak to that real quick? What is the difference between local and global?

DD: Well, I think local there is the perception at the very least and maybe a reality in some places that you can have control at least, you know, if you live in a city you have more direct access to the city council person, the school board member.

PG: And then when you move?

DD: When you move then maybe you have to set things up to have control there. I am just remembering for example we have the 3 strikes law that went into effect. We also had a situation where there was the possibility of it being over-turned, and at the time that the votes weren't there, there were 40% of the people who could vote who didn't vote; and when you go to any classroom, especially in the hood, and you ask people who knows somebody that's in jail that they are close to more than half the people raise their hands and I kept thinking well, unless we are busting guns to set everybody free, which we are not, unless we've got an army there we are getting prepared to really liberate them, which, at least from where I sit I don't see that, why allow ourselves to lose an election by less than 10% when we had 40% of the people who could vote, not vote.

PG: Because other than you, Michael Eric Dyson, Al Sharpton, Tavis Smiley, Chuck D. and a slew of others that I could mention no one is going into the hood teaching Tay-Tay and Man-Man these things. Puffy's not, Nellie ain't, Jermaine Dupree is not, they on TV talking about rock the vote. So what is voter registration without voter education? So, it's nice for you to say that to me, it may resonate fine with me, but how about the ones who have no education, don't know anything about the process is what I am talking about. Who is going to educate Tay-Tay and Man-Man and Re-Re in the projects to get them to understand the voting process? And then on the flip side of that, who is going to put a mental cap, an intellectual one in somebody's ass when they abuse that privilege and that seat..., no one. Thank you very much. This is Professor Griff, I'm here with Davey D. and we have to rock the bells backstage and we're signing out. It was very interesting interviewing you Davey D. and hopefully we can catch you some other time and ask you some very, very more important questions as the electoral process gets put in place and we see who is going to be the next President to be selected. This is

115

Professor Griff on site here at Rock the Bells, thank you very much. Peace.

DD: There we go. My man Griff has to get back and do his duties. I appreciate it man. We're out. Peace.

* *

New York City Jail Cell Downtown Manhattan- 1988

SET IT OFF!

Interview with Professor Griff 6/2006 09:00
by Kalonji Jama Changa Source www.tla-pronline.com
Public Enemy Rap Activist Talks Revolution with FTP Movement

In 1987 when Public Enemy stepped on the scene with their debut album, "Yo! Bumrush The Show," they shocked the world. No one knew they would be recognized as one of the most controversial groups in the history of rap. Now 12 albums later, millions of records sold and performances in over 40 countries, the group is still doing their thing with their latest release, Rebirth of a Nation, featuring West Coast rebel rap artist, Paris.

The group started out with the front man Chuck D, the side-show Flava Flav, Terminator X (DJ) and the Minister of Information and leader of the S1W's (Security of the First World), Professor Griff. Years before Flava Flav's infamous VH1 television stunts, another member of Public Enemy was at the center of controversy. In 1989, based on an interview with The Washington Post, Professor Griff, who was misquoted, was accused of anti-semitism and faced a barrage of attacks from the Jewish Community. During this time period, Professor Griff made headlines around the country and had several attempts on his life including a sniper attack and poisoning.

I first met Professor Griff in Atlanta after a lecture I gave. He then invited me to open up for his now classic discourse, "Strange Love, has Public Enemy lost its Flava." Since that particular engagement, we have shared the stage on several different panel discussions and lectures. A strong community activist, he has supported different programs that we have launched in Atlanta, including the Feed The People program and a joint benefit effort for Bernard Burden, a

victim of a lynching that took place a year and a half ago in the State
of Georgia.

On Friday June 2, 2006, I caught up with Professor Griff at Lush
Life Cafe in the West End of Atlanta and what followed was this
interview. Brace Yo' self!

Kalonji: In your words, what is revolution?

Professor Griff: When the term revolution is mentioned, nowadays
a lot of people look at it as a passé term. They only think of the
"negro" revolution that we had here in America. Although, some
Brothers, Sisters and a lot of organizations during the 60's, did bring
about change, it wasn't a complete, total, constructive, conscious
change. So when defining revolution, revolution is complete, total,
constructive, conscious change. When we look back on different
revolutions around the globe, for instance the Cuban Revolution
what kind of change did that bring about? It brought about a
complete, total, constructive, conscious change for the people in
Cuba - with Fidel Castro, Raul Castro and Che Guevara. When you
talk about Revolution, you're not talking about necessarily
overthrowing the physical government in the land in which we live
in, but overthrowing the government of your mind- so it has to be a
complete, constructive, conscious change. In a nutshell, that's what
revolution means to me. Every step you take towards that particular
goal is revolution, long as it's about change. The clinical definition
for insanity or insane is when you constantly do the same thing over
and over again and expect a different result. That's not gonna
happen, that's counter revolutionary...I think a lot of the things that
we're doing, such as what Tavis Smiley is doing with The Covenant
is counter revolutionary. Actually trying to take steps backwards in
order to go forward.

Kalonji: Do you feel we have effective Black Leadership in America
today, and if so who would you consider leadership?

Professor Griff: When you say effective leadership, I think Al
Sharpton put it best. He said, "We have those who call themselves
Black Leadership, or we could reverse that and say those who call

themselves leading Blacks." We have a lot of negroes that like to lead Blacks. They don't necessarily know where they're going but they wanna lead. So, if you're talking about using this system to lead Black People, then I think that's sad because this system is not designed to lead Black People anywhere. This system was constructed to keep Black People in a box and a certain place and those handpicked Black leaders are put in place to do just that. So when we talk about effective Black Leadership, what kind of change do they affect? Do they put policies in place that reach as high as the government and as low as the projects, that can affect Pookie, Man-man, Tay-Tay and Peanut? I don't think this is true. Other than the leadership of The Most Honorable Louis Farrakhan, I can't see anyone else being too effective. There's a Brother Ray Hagin (pastor), in St. Louis. There's a couple of other Brothers that have different organizations on a small scale they're reaching Grassroots people. But, you have 40 to 70 million Black People in America that need to be effected. So we need something broad across the board. A lot of us still believe in the exoteric, where we are waiting for someone to come save us, this whole Messiah concept, and that's played out. It's not gonna happen.

Kalonji: Earlier you mentioned the whole 60's Movement, Do you feel there is a Movement right now and if there is what is that Movement missing in 2006?

Professor Griff: Yes, I think there are different Movements that are going on. Things are moving and things are changing, but I don't think there is a common thread - I don't think we are moving as a whole. I think Chuck D said it better, he said, "We move as a team, we never move alone /the posse is ready and we operating in our zone." So were moving, you're moving. There are different organizations across the globe that are moving. Different Revolutionary Organizations are moving a lot of people. Is there a common thread there? Do we have the basics of economics - which is Land? No. We don't feed ourselves, someone else feeds us. We don't clothe ourselves. We don't educate ourselves. We get these things from someone else. Therefore that leadership we talked about is ineffective. That Movement and that change that we need that so called moving the masses of our people, will not be successful if the basics are not taken care of. The basic things that our people should do for themselves.

Kalonji: What's your take on Voting? About two years ago cats like Puff and Russell were pushing this whole Vote or Die thing. What do you think about that, are we gonna Vote and still Die or what's the deal?

Professor Griff: I think Malcolm said it best when he gave us the analogy of "The Ballot or The Bullet." I think we should look at the whole Vote or Die as being some kind of scheme using negroes like Puffy to come lock down that whole demographic from 18 to 35. Even if you did vote, who would you vote for? Do those particular candidates come to the hood to speak to us? Number 2, if you are going to register people to vote, why not have a voter education to educate the people on the policies and the agendas of the candidates. Then we need to look at the long term effects of what voting does, where do those registration cards go? I know for a fact that the Selective Draft Services of the United States Government uses those cards to choose who is selected for the draft from the voter registration cards. That's very important. That's something we need to know and we don't know that. What has voting ever done for us? Vote or Die? No. That's a charade, that's a trick. You got imps like Chuck D to fall into things like that, because he the main one on TV, talkin' bout, we need to vote. MTV Rock The Vote, with that kind of madness! That vote is a scam Bro, and you and I know it and they should know it also.

Kalonji: You know I agree with that...You mentioned some Hip Hop artists, you're coming from Public Enemy, one of the most popular groups in the History of Hip Hop. Do you think Hip Hop artists should be held accountable for their music and do they have a responsibility to help build the Black community?

Professor Griff: In dealing with Hip Hop and lyrical content, there definitely comes a social responsibility along with that. This question and this answer may not fit every artist in every genre in music. But, it does with Black People simply because there are no other people on the face of the Earth in the particular situation we're in. I can't

121

even include the Brothers and Sisters on the Continent. They are not in the situation we're in. They did not lose their Name, Culture, and God. They probably lost a few other things, but we were the ones that were knocked over the head and dragged to America and lost everything. So we do have a social responsibility along with the lyrical content. I can't go out here and make a shoot'em up bang-bang kind of video. Shoot'em up bang-bang kind of songs, the rims are spinnin', I'm bling-blinggin' and these kind of songs and not be held accountable for the effect that it has on the hood. A lot of times we come up outta these situations and we talk about those same situations "about keepin' it real" at the age of 17 - 18 years old. How come 10-15 years will go by and we 30 still talkin' about the same situation. Especially those that are in Hip Hop that are millionaires. You wearing a $100,000 in each ear, you got a $200,000 grill, a million dollar pinky ring and about $400,000 on ya wrist and you still talkin' bout what Pookie, Man-man and Tay-Tay are doing in the projects? Naw, something is wrong with that man. You should be the one comin' out of the projects and now that you are quote-unquote successful, you should be going back laying out some kind of economic game plan because someone did it for you.

Kalonji: Bubba Sparxxx has a video for a song called "Ms. New Booty," with a lot of Sistahs "shakin' what they mama gave 'em"...Do you feel it's artistry or exploitation? Do you feel the people should support someone like Bubba Sparxxx or do you feel that he is capitalizing off of the Sistahs?

Professor Griff: Most definitely he's capitalizing off of the ignorance of the people. But, ignorant is not a bad word, ignorant just means you choose to ignore, so it's not like these people don't know. We can go back in history and look at that same kind of scene being played out. The white rap artist talking about the Ma, The Mother and even with Black rap artists who constantly attack the womb. The micro-womb not the macro-womb. The smaller womb because they don't respect the macro-womb of the Universe. We attack the Womb as if we didn't come from the Womb like we came from somewhere else, so we attack the Ma, which is the Great Mother. Not only that, in us attacking the Womb, we allow our open enemy to attack the Womb. Because his woman is not full figured and shaped like a real woman should, we allow these people to come over the fence and snatch our women. A lot of these women gladly go, as you seen in the video. That scene was played out with Janet Jackson allowing Justin Timberlake to rip her clothing off, exposing her breast. For some strange reason (some) Black Women feel that they have to please the slave masters children. Then us as Black Men sit on the sideline and allow it to go down. We don't chastise the woman, nor deal with the white man. Then again we on the world stage like punks once again. Unable to protect our women, unable to protect our children and until we stand up and do so....Probably at the detriment of being cursed out by the woman, but so-d_mn what! We have to take our rightful place. We can't do that with his woman. Imagine you going across the fence and snatching up a Jewish woman, calling her all kinds of b_tch_s and hoes on TV, you know Jewish people ain't having that. Imagine you snatching up a Jewish woman and calling her a kike, they will string yo' Black ass up downtown somewhere and tar and feather you. Right or wrong? So why should we allow it? In a minute some of us are going to get together and visit people like Bubba Sparxxx and we are going to talk to him. Talk to him (laughs)....

Kalonji: I hope you call me when it's time to talk (laughs). During the early 90's the Jewish community was upset about something you supposedly said. I heard that there was supposedly a hit out on you and there was actually a sniper from one particular Jewish organization on the roof at The Def Jam Building. Can you touch on that?

Professor Griff: I think just like any other Revolutionary trying to bring about a change with the people, especially a mental revolution, your own people are gonna want to fight you. Then you are going to get those who want to keep this thing on a hush, keep this thing as business as usual. Yeah, we gotta fight them also. There was an article in the paper (I still have the article) about how there was a Jewish gentlemen from the ADL across from RUSH Management company, on Elizabeth Street, Downtown Manhattan, shooting at the building. Thinking I was in there. They arrested him, and he did time. But you don't hear this stuff in the news, because our lives are not worth that much to people. This is not news worthy. So what another rapper dies. So they don't get it out to the masses of our people to the point where it hits us in the heart and we respond. We have been desensitized. That's just another nigga dead for them and for us it's business as usual, and we just push right along.

Kalonji: I heard you speak about our open enemy who would you say is our "open enemy?"

Professor Griff: When I say open enemy, Ava Muhammad taught us that everything in nature has an open enemy, a natural enemy. If we just stop and watch the Discovery Channel tonight, you can tell who is the enemy of the rat? It's the cat. Who is the open enemy of the cat? It's the dog. The open enemy of the chicken is the chicken hawk. So, if we look at white people's history and Black people's history and put them side by side, who is the open enemy of the Black Man and Woman? Who is the open enemy of God, it's the devil. That's easy to tell! But, you will get some negro, babblin' on TV, like Michael Eric Dyson or "Corny" West or one of them, who will try to intellectualize this. Rather than come out and say, because they're scared, they're punks. They fear the open enemy. But you can't tell that to Amilcar Cabral, you can't tell that to different revolutionaries, because we know the enemy. You can't say that to Steve Biko, Che Guevara, we know and understand who the enemy is. You can't tell that to Kalonji Jama Changa. You can't tell that to Fred Hampton Jr., you know what I'm saying? I had the pleasure of doing a lecture in New Jersey and guess who walked in the door? Dr. Leonard Jefferies. I was like Wow! One of the Elders sitting in my lecture! I felt honored. You can't tell that to a Brother like that, who knows who the open enemy is, who goes back to Egypt every year and tells us who the open enemy is. It wasn't no secret then, and it ain't no secret now.

Kalonji: In your lectures you often talk about the "scared to death negro." What is a scared to death negro?

Professor Griff: Let's define negro as a human being who has been written off as being dead. Negro coming from the Latin word meaning, black, dead, lifeless. A black shoe, a black board, a black tire, dead, lifeless. Let's see who some of the scared to death negroes are. Let's look at all the Black Mayors without even naming names. Let's roll off the idea of you being a Black Mayor in a "Black city." As many Mayors as we ran through in the past 10 years you would think we own or runnin' something, you would think we coming up. Not the case. We not runnin' anything in America, but our mouths. So, when I say scared to death negroes, not those brave men and women that are in Congress, that's working in cities I go to, that help Black people raise their conscious level to help Black people do something for the masses of our people. Not them. The ones that wanna take the lead and have no platform, that wanna take the lead and lead us right back to the slave masters plantation. We got some scared to death negroes that are rappers, that are really sitting comfortable. I heard recently that cats like Nelly are vegetarians, so why not make a song and help the masses of the people get up off this swine, this pork, this pig? No you would rather keep making these kind of songs to keep the people in the same wretched condition there in? That's sad, somebody need to come see you. Harriet Tubman dealt with that scared to death negro, like we dealing with that scared to death negro today. There's a railroad of bones that you can trace back and follow right back to the Continent of Africa. There's dead dry bones here in America, all throughout the 9,000 miles it took us to get here and there are dead dry bones there of our Ancestors. So for you not to remember this and not stand on the shoulders of those who came before us, you a scared to death negro! But, I say scared of what? You gonna die of something someday. I always tell people, I'm not gonna die on my knees, I am gonna die on my feet like a real man, standing up fighting this enemy.

Kalonji: The 1 Million Dollar Question....If I don't ask you this question we didn't do an interview...

Professor Griff: Let me answer it without you even asking. You about to ask me something about Flava?

Kalonji: You are absolutely correct.

Professor Griff: First of all we need to start the answer off like this, every Black Man in America needs to eat, whether you are in the rap game or not. We not gonna knock the next man's hustle on how you gotta eat. But dude, you're Public Enemy! We were the same one's talking about Bring The Noise, Don't Believe The Hype, Fight The Power. We were the same ones to talk about a Mind Revolution. Riot Starter, Public Enemy #1, Can't Trust It, Prophets of Rage! How could you now turn around and sweetheart the devil on TV? Lickin' and kissing on this white woman. There is a new generation that's coming up that never heard anything about Public Enemy. They heard glimpses about what Public Enemy was about, but in full they don't know what Public Enemy was about. These young people are coming up and seeing what Public Enemy is about thru the eyes of a cat like Flava Flav. Through madness of what he is doing on TV. We love the Brotha, very brilliant Brotha, very talented Brotha. But will he use his awareness to raise the masses of our people. Flava gotta eat, but it's just that we need to put some conscious thinking into what we do before we allow our open enemy to put this before the world. To continue to destroy us as a people. You know how many people watched one episode, of those 10 episodes that Flava did with Bridgette Nielsen on Strange Love? How many people it reached that's looking at Public Enemy like them cats sold out? Millions! That's a reality. If Flava Flav don't know it by now, and I'm sure this message will get to him, I did a 2 hour lecture, "Strange Love, has Public Enemy lost its Flava". Trying to lay it out and lay my position out, that we are not tolerating that. We need to stop sweet hearting the slave masters children. Now, I'm gonna put something out there that may be detrimental to a lot of people. Back in the days, I think all of us have had encounters with white women and white men. But, see we dealt with them in a different kind of way. I know when I was growing up, we did. If we ever dealt with a cracker, we were using her or getting something else. We don't deal with them like that now. We having children with them, we even marrying these devils, man. Which is Ridiculous! No, we should never, love the devil. Under no circumstance, he is not to be trusted especially with weakening your Melanin. You giving that Chemical Blackness, that life force away. This is what they live for. They trying to sneak into Heaven and we ain't allowing it.

Tavis Smiley- 2008

STILL STANDING
TAVIS SMILEY
Original airdate August 15, 2007

Professor Griff has long been an outspoken activist. Raised in Long Island, NY, he became a martial arts enthusiast and provided martial training for young people. He went on to form a security service, which led to his role as Minister of Information for the revolutionary hip-hop group, Public Enemy, which is celebrating its 20th year on the rap scene. Griff has also released a number of solo albums and supports a variety of programs, including Feed the People in the Atlanta, GA area, where he now lives.

Tavis: This makes you feel old. It's hard to believe it's been 20 years since Public Enemy came crashing into the national consciousness with their brilliant debut album "Yo, Bum Rush the Show." One year later, of course, came an even bigger record featuring classic and powerful songs like "Don't Believe the Hype."

Twenty years later, they are still making thought-provoking and relevant music. Out now with their new disc - bam, there it is - "How You Sell Soul to a Soulless People Who Sold Their Soul." See, you can't (unintelligible) PE. (Laughter) Before we get into the new disc, here is some classic PE back in the day – "Public Enemy Number One."

Tavis: Flavor Flav. I was watching a roast of him on Comedy Central the other night - you see any of that, Griff?

Professor Griff: Yes, sir. Yeah.

Tavis: Funny stuff.

Chuck D: I don't watch Comedy Central.

Tavis: You don't watch Comedy Central?

Chuck D: No, I made a promise that I would do a thing for him, and it was in another city on another day, and I heard they attached it.

Tavis: It is what it is.

Chuck D: You know what it is; we boil it down to us. It's like, it's that every Black family always got that one person. (Laughter) I don't care -

Griff: You can't deny it.

Chuck D: And even when White folks say it in America, I say, "Oh, you done forgot that there was Billy Carter, huh?"

Tavis: Yeah, yeah, yeah. Or Paris Hilton and the Hilton family. You're right, every family has one.

Chuck D: Yeah, he's that one.

Tavis: Let me take you back to the beginning. When the group was formed -

Chuck D: You say we were wearing white, so I guess we lost our musical virginity or something.

Tavis: Yeah. (Laughter) What was Flavor bringing to the table?

Chuck D: Greatest hype man ever in the history - he invented the (unintelligible). And -

Griff: I think on top of that, a lot of times in most cases the people we were trying to reach would not gravitate towards I guess the dynamic between me and Chuck. Born on the same day, same hospital, the whole bit. Same -

Tavis: That's true?

Griff: Yes.

Tavis: Wow.

Griff: So, we bring a certain kind of energy. Flavor drew all of those people that we could never reach. So he drew them to us and we got a chance to at least interact with them, to raise a conscious level.

Tavis: Of course I should have - you know this already, you PE fans - the guy on the left with the hat would happen to be Chuck D. And of course, Professor Griff sitting nearest me on the set.

Chuck D: We're a group. We let people know very quickly, like, we're a group and we think the essence of Black music - especially rap music and hip-hop - is groups. And somehow in the nineties and the millennium, groups have been forsaken and have been forgotten for this whole individual (inaudible) -

Tavis: What's behind that, you think?

Chuck D: Well I think the thing is our travels around the world, traveling to 60 countries together, seeing many people, many places, and a lot of things.

Tavis: But what do you think, Griff, if Chuck is right - and he is right about that - that rap has moved from - back in the day, we could run a litany of them - there were so many groups back in the day; now there are individuals. What's behind that, you think?

Griff: The whole idea of creating an icon, an idol to worship, to follow. The whole idea of the super-size me mentality. It's all about me, the I, the me, me, me society. It's all in that individual. Constantly writing and talking about and praying about the acquisition of wealth, and it's all about me. The bigger the car. You kind of figure 300 million people in this country, how many cars are there? About 300 million. (Laughter) Do you understand what I'm saying? So that speaks to it.

Chuck D: And the HOV lanes are rarely packed.

Griff: Ain't that something? (Inaudible) bike lane, HOV lane.

Tavis: Where did the commitment come from to saying something in the music? To the point now about being individual, it's not always about saying anything. But where did the commitment come on the part of the group to actually saying something with your music?

Chuck D: Simple, we evolved out of the sixties, and from the Curtis Mayfield's, the James Brown, Aretha Franklins, the last poets and people that put it down in the sixties, we're children from that. And then this guy's one of the first DJs I ever witnessed in the middle of the seventies, playing some of those same records.

Tavis: What do you make now, looking back - first of all, are you feeling like it's been 20 years? Are you feeling that?

Chuck D: No, not at all. When people talk about 20 years, it's a benchmark in rap music and hip-hop. But one thing we came along understanding that we have to be musicologists. And being a musicologist comes out of the understanding that this comes out of records. Afrika Bambaataa, Kool Herc, and Grandmaster Flash all were DJs that understood not only (unintelligible) DXT are DJs that not only understood the record but the musicians inside the records.

And the record companies, they even might have exploited them. Our understanding is this understanding that there's a homage to the musicians and the records, and in knowing that blues artists have

131

gotten down 50 years. BB King is still doing his thing. The holy trinity, or better yet the founding fathers of rock and roll - Chuck Berry, Little Richard, Fats Domino - are not only here today but they're doing gigs.

And often by our people, because history is not this thing that we feel that's a part of us that we should search and seek. We've lost the fact that these brothers are still here, sisters are still here doing what they innovated on long ago.

Tavis: But see, Griff, that's what makes for me this conversation so profound, because getting to a 20-year benchmark in the hip-hop is, like, unheard of. There's so few people who hit a 20-year mark where their music is still relevant, where their work, where their witness is still relevant, where folks still want to hear from them - they still want to hear what Chuck has to say, what Griff has to say.

Even to your point about Flav - Flav, 20 years later, is still putting it down in his own way on television and getting people to tune in to watch his insaneness and his craziness. But he's making his thing work. The question behind that is how in the hip-hop world do you stay relevant for 20 years? It's, like, unheard of?

Griff: I think there's some things that lend to that particular dynamic. One, I think we have the ability to speak outside of the CD, like we're doing now. He's been on the lecture circuit; I've been on the lecture circuit, so we can speak outside of the CD because the songs are relevant. I think, too, Prince called this music that we're hearing today - and it's not hip-hop; we call it something else - disposable music.

It's like a piece of bubblegum. You buy it, chew it, spit it out and that's it. Hopefully it don't get stuck to the bottom of your shoe. So it's bubblegum music, and a lot of times when there's no substance in the music, it has no longevity. The average CDs stay in the shelf how long? Maybe three weeks? And I defy anyone in your listening audience, name me the number one single last year this time.

It's very difficult to do, because we don't remember. It don't stick to the ribs. Now, that time that my old uncle was giving my car the tune-up and teaching me how to do that, I remember Sly and the Family Stone, James Brown, Curtis Mayfield, Gladys Knight and the Pips. You understand? Because those things stuck to the ribs.

Tavis: Let's be honest about this - you could not have had - maybe being the visionary that you are, Chuck, maybe you did, I don't know - but I can't imagine you guys could have had any idea when you guys formed this group over 20 years ago now, that you would be regarded by "The New York Times," by "Rolling Stone" - every major publication in the country has listed something that you have done on their top 20 list of all time this, their top 50 list of all time that.

Did you ever have any idea that the impact that you were going to bring to the game would be so profound and recognized, even by mainstream?

Chuck D: We knew the music would be very powerful for years to come, and we expected that there would be other situations outside the music that would delve into the music and also direct it in a whole bunch of different places. We didn't necessarily know our place, and it wasn't self-serving to look at our place. Like, this is who we are.

But we knew where we had came from and what had actually turned us on as young people to actually infuse inside rap music and hip-hop. But I would tell you this - that the saving grace for Public Enemy is that we never relied on the United States of America to be our sole base. We always relied that there is a Black Diaspora; there is a struggle amongst people around the planet that we could learn about and align ourselves with and attach to our music.

And we knew that once we got our passports - although I even think passports are derogatory, knowing that you need permission to go somewhere else on the planet, the one place that God gave you - we used them. And up to this point, 20 years, Public Enemy has frequented 60 countries. And we've frequented not only 60 countries but the cities and the realms of societies within. And hearing a lot of stories from thousands of people and understanding that our place is as citizens of the planet, and not just exactly where we come from.

Tavis: What's the response, Griff, when you travel around the world, and what have you most taken from the opportunity to travel to these 60 countries over the years?

Griff: We're discovering that regardless of your complexion, regardless of your nationality or your race, we're finding people all over the globe have the same struggle as Black people in America - just on a different level. And it's critical, because, as he said, we travel to - this is almost our what, 60th tour and it's like in the beginning, we didn't know people was going to understand what we were doing. It was new to us.

So to go to Amsterdam, go to London, Germany, Europe and a lot of the place, and it's, like, amazing to see people really, truly understand. Maybe not every nuance, everything that we were saying, but they understood the frequency in the music and they understood it spoke to something in them. And the same thing that was going on in their life was going on in our lives in America - just on a different level, that's all.

Tavis: When you see that and you come back and you prepare for the next project, it informs your music, it informs your work in what way?

Griff: I think in the way we're a lot more cautious when we put the pen to the pad, because now scope is broader, and now we know if we're going back to some of these same places we have to incorporate the people's struggle. Not only the local and national level, but global now.

Tavis: I want to talk about the new CD here in a second. Let me just throw some hits at you, and you tell me anything about the hit, anything connected to it you want to tell me.

Chuck D: Are they hits? (Laughter) We ain't had no hits.

Tavis: You had hits, man, no, no, no, no. You tell me - we all know the music, but you tell me the story behind the music. When we all listen to "Fight the Power," and still listen and love it to this day - tell me about "Fight the Power."

Griff: That was a crazy day in Brooklyn.

Chuck D: Yeah, theme for "Do The Right Thing," Spike said he needed an anthem. We did a tour with Run-DMC, came back with an anthem. But more importantly, I think we were inspired by the Isley Brothers in 1975, who came up with the same slogan. You gotta fight the powers that be; you just can't sit down.

Tavis: What did the exposure of that song on that soundtrack do for the group?

Griff: One of two things. It put us in a position where we had to define who the powers that be are.

Chuck D: The forces at work.

Griff: Right. So in defining that, I think - like I said earlier, it gave us the opportunity to speak outside of the song.

Tavis: Go back to the beginning – "It Takes a Nation of Millions."

Chuck D: It takes a nation of millions to hold us back is actually a line from the first record, a song called "Raise the Roof." And it was something I saw in print when I described that song, and it was in Toronto. And Hank Shockley said, "Hey, I think that could be the name of the title of the album," and that's what it is. It was twofold -

135

it could take a nation of millions to hold us back as adversaries, or it takes a nation of millions of us to hold ourselves back.

And I think where we're at in 007, which is 2007, is really when we go around the world; it's easy to recognize forces at work here against us. Dead Prez comes up with a campaign against corporations, its turn off the radio. Professor Griff has turn off channel zero. And he can explain that. There's a lot of things manipulating Black people's imagery right about now that we always have to be the anti-force at work, to work against that. Not to say that we're going to change and flip things overnight, but if you lie down you'll fall for anything.

Tavis: Turn off channel zero, since Chuck went there, is what, Griff?

Griff: It's a project that me and about 20 to 25 activists across the country put together a documentary film dealing with the negative images in the media. And we just put it out free to give it to organizations and groups and teachers and preachers and leaders to have discussions about it, to raise the consciousness level of the people.

Tavis: Since you're on that, tell me what PE's role has been over the 20 years, vis-à-vis the music, in trying to address this issue of Black images in media.

Griff: I think bottom line it could be said best - probably not best, but from my perspective, we've become the voice of the voiceless in areas where a lot of people just won't go. We pride ourselves in reaching (unintelligible) and Peanut in the projects, and Re-Re. (Laughter) So being, a lot of people labeled us because of the song "The Prophets of Rage," but that's another subject. But we became the voice of the voiceless.

Tavis: One more song title - "911 Is a Joke in Your Town."

Chuck D: Healthcare and it responded to the non-response of services in our community. I gave Flavor the title. I said, "You got a year to write this rap." (Laughter)

Tavis: It took a whole year and a half.

Chuck D: And he came back, yeah. So yeah, there's a lot of things that happened in that, there's misconceptions about Public Enemy in this realm because we don't get the media balance that's necessary. But we thank you for allowing the media balance. There's a big yin to the yang that they kind of see every day.

Tavis: You believe that - I assume you do; everything you say, you believe - you really believe that there is a lack of balance in the coverage of PE? And I say that only because -

Chuck D: In this country?

Tavis: Yeah.

Chuck D: Yeah.

Tavis: Tell me why you feel that. Because PE is so celebrated, as I said earlier, by all these publications for the impact that you've had over the last 20 years.

Chuck D: I think Griff can speak to that.

Griff: I don't know, but if you look at it on a psychological level, you don't think in some cases on the other side of the fence Public Enemy is being neutralized? Because we don't look at it like we're getting the play that a lot of the other groups get that are actually talking about absolutely nothing.

Chuck D: Also I would say that this is, like, when it comes down to other frivolous expression, I think they realize that they have to repeat it over and over and over again. And when you say something that's pertinent it might enter the realm, like, once. Just like I tell

137

people that history is taught to you. And maybe your history might be taught to you, but it's taught to you so quickly if you don't grab onto it and keep it and apply it to yourself, it's out of sight, out of mind.

But dumb*ish*, as we say, keep coming at you over and over again. And just like Viacom - and I blame Viacom and maybe the VH1 station. Flavor is Flavor - he's been the same dude forever. He's been the same guy. But they saw some DNA in there where they said, "Wow, we can go into that and we can just mass produce it and just repeat it over and over again." And yes, it's entertainment; it might make you laugh.

But not everything is funny. But a corporation only measures us as a people by our quantity and not our quality. And I'm always looking at the system and saying, more doesn't always mean better, just because you have millions versus thousands. I look at the quality of the thousands and the millions before I say that's better.

We're still on an archaic voting system which says either you gotta be in this party or that party, and at the end of the day the one with the most wins. How primitive is that? So we as hip-hop artists have always delved into the under spoken or unspoken by saying we want to be able to have the music and the art form actually get into areas where credit has not been due.

Yes, it's entertaining; yes, it could be funny. But where's the adherence for hip-hop to be respected for the changes it can do in education, for the changes it can do just in social order? Where's the communication for people who have been I guess incarcerated in the prison industrial complex? There's a lot of movements that have been going on, have been raised on hip-hop, but hip-hop has not had that accepted portal of acceptance for people to say, "Hey, wow, this is a wonderful basis that I've learned from."

Griff: But I think multinational corporations understand that dynamic.

138

Chuck D: Oh, of course.

Griff: And they also understand that younger people that would have respected Public Enemy, see Public Enemy through the eyes of a Flavor Flav show, and that may hurt instead of help.

Tavis: To your point, and this is much bigger than Flavor, because as we've said Flav's been that way all the way through and somebody saw something and then wanted to exploit that. But what do we say to those persons, though, on MTV - those personalities, that is to say, on MTV, on VH1, God knows on BET - what do we say to those personalities that allow that to happen?

They can't exploit something if there isn't something to exploit, so there are a lot of folk who are stepping up and volunteering, quite frankly, to be exploited in that way.

Chuck D: I think it boils down to us being able to say that this is something that we'll do versus something that we say that we won't do. And a lot of personalities, they know that they have to have their job or whatever. But then also there's other people that have their own grassroots operations that need some airtime that need to be respected, as well.

And we have always said that we are a diverse community. And there's a lot of things going on all at once, but everything is just not synonymously just a one-trick type of way of living. So, there's artists that will just be artists. There's entertainers that will just be entertainers, and that will be all that they will do. But when it comes down to us as Black folks, we've been involved in so many different areas in managements and companies and distributions and publishing's that will never get the light that other situations have.

That's why we call ourselves the Rolling Stones of the rap game. If they got (unintelligible) about Mick and Keith for their 40 years in rock and roll, they gotta talk about us and our 20 years in the rap music and hip-hop game.

Griff: And I think that if they knew better, they would do better. And I think a lot of them know. And those, the ones that do know and are not trying to help the situation, eventually we have to bring them to the table of accountability at any, all, and every means necessary.

Tavis: Tell me about the new CD, Chuck. This title, first of all. I love this title.

Chuck D: Well, "How You Sell Soul to a Soulless People Who Sold Their Soul -" matter of fact, you don't. (Laughter) You can't. My thing, I tell people hey, you can get the music however way you got it, but this is pretty much telling people if you don't know what soul is, and if you kind of said you don't want to do something based on your inner self, then maybe you should be introduced to soul to recognize it.

We give people the option. We say, "You could support us if you want; we're still going to do our thing." So we're not telling people to go out and buy our album. It's there, along with 14 other albums, and we might be in the town to do what we do. But we say that the business in this - the record industry is in trouble; the music industry is not.

We're in the music industry, which means that we tell people, I say, choose between the two. Because a company coming to people saying buy, buy, buy, buy, buy all the time has met its end. You can't beg people where the basic necessities are food, shelter, and clothing and tell them that they gotta buy a music offering.

Tavis: I like that distinction, though, between the record industry being in trouble and the music industry not being in trouble.

Griff: We make songs every day, regardless of whether they end up on an album or not.

Tavis: In terms of what's on the CD, how does this fit into the pantheon of the other countless albums ya'll have done?

Chuck D: It just fits. (Laughter)

Tavis: It just fits, huh?

Griff: It's not a progressive thing or a left or a right thing; it just kind of fits because - well, you said you dug the title. When studying the soul, don't you know soul records that move your soul?

Chuck D: So there's some - you know Gary Gee Whiz, one of the members of the original Bomb Squad. The Bomb Squad has kind of expanded to 15 to 16 producers in this digital age; Griff is one of them. DJ Johnny Juice, Gary Gee Whiz did this one with (unintelligible) Smith. So the lead single is called "Harder Than You Think," and simply, it's like to be progressive, proactive, and positive is harder than you think. (Laughter) But that don't mean that you don't do it.

Tavis: Church said amen on that. And ya'll don't play, either - 19 tracks on one CD.

Chuck D: It's not the quantity; it's the quality. (Laughter)

Griff: The 19 is a very significant number; we'll deal with that later.

Chuck D: There we go, there we go. (Laughter)

Tavis: Nineteen is a - before I let you go, our dear friend - our mutual friend, Dr. Cornel West and I were doing a joint lecture the other day, and in the middle of this lecture we referenced you; something you said the last time I saw you, and it fit perfectly into the speech to these young people. That I'd rather be - how'd Chuck D put it?

I'd rather be hated for what I am than loved for what I'm not.

Chuck D: Than loved for what I'm not.

Tavis: That's (unintelligible).

141

Chuck D: That came from Big Daddy Kane's album.

Griff: We have to give big shout-outs (unintelligible) family.

Tavis: (Unintelligible) you just did.

Chuck D: Yeah.

Griff: And his passing, we have to remember that he's one of those brothers, those icons in the community that put it down in the educational department and stand on his shoulders - (unintelligible).

Chuck D: Yes.

Tavis: He did do that.

Griff: Yes.

Tavis: PE - been around 20 years now. The new CD, "How You Sell Soul to a Soulless People Who Sold Their Soul."

Chuck D: And they could go to PublicEnemy.com or MySpace/PublicEnemy.

Tavis: And the answer is, you don't. (Laughter) But get the CD, because it has 19 tracks on it, and 19 is a very significant number.

Chuck D: And the DVD. We release DVDs on every one of our albums.

Tavis: CD and DVD - can't (unintelligible) PE. First of all, let me close by saying thank you. That's all I can say.

Griff: Give thanks, yes, sir.

Tavis: Thank you for all that ya'll have done and continue to do.

Chuck D: Thanks, Mr. T.

Tavis: Love you both.

Chuck D: All right.

Tavis: That's our show for tonight.

Public Enemy, Professor Griff, Sunshine Theater, Albuquerque, New Mexico
David Scheinbaum, 2002

ONE GOD ONE NATION
PROFESSOR GRIFF
AHK AL MUMIN- PART 1 (September 16, 2008)

Muhammad Speaks Newspaper of the Lost-Found Nation of Islam under the Leadership of the Honorable Silis Muhammad, CEO, interviewed Professor Griff at the Grounds Coffeehouse @ West End in Atlanta.

Al Mumin: As Saalam Alaikum Brother.

Professor Griff: Wa Alaikum Salaam

Al Mumin: Thank you for doing this interview for Muhammad Speaks Newspaper and for letting us film it. Please tell us a little background about yourself.

Professor Griff: You're welcome brother. Well, that's a long story. I am my father's son, his 7th son from a family of 13. I am the 12th child. Born and raised in Long Island New York. Had a normal upbringing. It was kind of difficult for my mom with that many children. You can imagine, scraping the bottom of the cereal box, but nonetheless, very peaceful on long island. We didn't catch a lot of things that were going on, Bronx Brooklyn, Queens, Manhattan. But, uhm, yeah just went away to school upstate New York in Rochester; 9th or 10th grade, went to East High School. That's where I first got familiar with some of the teachings of the Most Honorable Elijah Muhammad. But it wasn't until I came back, end of the 10th or 11th grade; my two brothers were in the Nation of Islam. Kind of got introduced and then figured that was in the first resurrection,

1973, '74. From there joined a few revolutionary organizations. Went through the Cadets; ended up joining the military as a military police, ended up being a correctional specialist. Came back out, hit the streets with that kind of knowledge, started putting together a couple of underground organizations; which led into Unity Force, which led into the S1 W's, which led to hooking up with Chuck, Flav, Bomb Squad, Terminator X to do the whole Public Enemy thing. So in a nutshell, that's pretty much it.

Al Mumin: So now you said you hooked up with the crew of Public Enemy?

Professor Griff: Well, not really. They weren't Public Enemy then.

Al Mumin: So you just pretty much knew them as individuals at that time?

Professor Griff: Right, and uhm, it was one of those situations where I was hooked up with Hank Shockley, Keith Shockley, and Jerry J. We had a crew called Spectrum City and we were DJ's. It was Chuck who joined us.

Al Mumin: And where was this at?

Professor Griff: Long Island, New York; roughly around '80, '81, '82.

Al Mumin: So, did you kind of meet at friend's houses or some organizations?

Professor Griff: Naw. In Roosevelt, that's kinda corny man. If you lived in Roosevelt, then you had to know everybody in Roosevelt. Roosevelt is only one square mile. Dr. J, a couple of members of Guy, Eddie Murphy, Charlie Murphy, all of us from Roosevelt.

Al Mumin: So how did the group form, Public Enemy?

Professor Griff: Well, that was pretty much the formation of Public Enemy. We use to do these parties man, like you know the Korean Ballroom and other places. Since I had the crew, the Unity Force, the soldiers; Chuck was a graphic artist, cause he was at Delphi University, and Hank was connected as a DJ through Spectrum City and through college radio. We just came together and started doing parties – with, remember Dre and Ed Lover, from MTV? We just hooked up with them so.....

Al Mumin: So what were the early years like when you all formed?

Professor Griff: Bill Stephanie at Delphi, Hank Shockley and Chuck having discussions with Rick Ruben, Jam Master J, Russell Simmons, you know that was the early beginnings as far as Public Enemy as far as the recordings. I think Hank Shockley and Chuck can best tell that story and Bill Stephanie.

Al Mumin: Well, I heard, hearsay of course, not directly from any of the members or yourself, that there was some controversy. You had made some statements, things like that uhm.

Professor Griff: Hell, there's always controversy. Which part, which aspect of the controversy?

Al Mumin: Was there a split over a Jewish issue you were talking about?

Professor Griff: I think the split occurred at the peak of information getting out about who controls the music industry and since I was the minister of information, and I was the one to tell it, I guess the weight fell back on me. I call it a bright day, not a dark day, but a bright day in Public Enemy's history because that shed some light on who's really in control.

Al Mumin: So what happened after that?

Professor Griff: I think at the behest of some people outside of the context of Public Enemy, I think Chuck was put in a position where he felt it was better to let me go rather than stand up and defend the statements.

Al Mumin: So now in the present day are you all reunited again?

Professor Griff: We cool, but the issue surrounding the statements is resolved? I don't think so. Until we stand up as men and say to ourselves who really controls the music industry, and lay it out for the world to see that issue is not going to be resolved. That's like someone coming in your house and coming between you and your wife, and you all pretend like this big, fat, black, ugly elephant is not sitting in your living room when he's smelling up the place. You understand what I'm saying? But until you recognize, both you and your wife recognize that there is an elephant in the room that we need to get rid of. But as long as you keep ignoring it and acting like the elephant ain't there, trying to use the remote to change the channel on the TV, and your wife keeps telling you, "sweetheart, honey, we got to get rid of this elephant in the living room!" and we act like the elephant ain't even there! When we know it's there. We gotta pay the rent to the elephant, we gotta feed the elephant, we gotta make sure the elephant is not making too much noise. You understand what I'm saying?

Al Mumin: So you're basically on cool terms but you're doing your own separate things?

Professor Griff: We have to look past individual feelings, because Public Enemy is a lot larger than my feelings. It's a lot larger than Chuck and Flavor Flav.

Al Mumin: I know you're a busy man. Can you tell us some activities you're currently involved in, and what is your mission as far as our people are concerned?

Professor Griff: I think the mission throughout what I've done thus far spells itself out. We have to raise the consciousness level of our people by any, every and all means necessary. We must not shirk in our responsibility and our duty in doing this. I'm just doing mine through the medium of music, other than just doing lectures and raising the awareness of the people, I teach martial arts, free of charge, women's self defense class because I believe women should learn self defense to protect the babies. I'm involved in certain activities I can't mention on camera, but nonetheless, still educating people and still creating opportunities for people to come to sit down in seminars and lectures to raise their consciousness level. You understand what I'm saying? That's basically where I'm at. You know a lot of the strategies we can't put out there. Because not only are we watching this, but our open enemy is watching this, so we have to understand that.

Al Mumin: I just wanted to inform my people, make them aware without compromising our position....

Professor Griff: Yeah, well, now a days in 2008, our people have to meet us half-way. You understand what I'm saying? We have a saying in revolutionary circles, "All those who know, know."

Al Mumin: The next question is, "what do you think of the Nation of Islam and when I ask that, inside of that, about Master Fard Muhammad, The Honorable Elijah Muhammad, Wallace D. Muhammad, Minister Louis Farrakhan, and Mr. Muhammad?"

Professor Griff: Right. I think the Nation of Islam is just what it says it is. It is a Nation of Islam. And I encourage every audience that I speak in front of to stop thinking as individuals but start acting as though we are a nation; we are a nation of peace; we're an organized group of individuals who have brought our families together under one banner, one flag, one ideology, one philosophy, one God one aim one purpose, one destiny. I think all of the Muhammad's are doing a marvelous work. But to separate Silas from Wallace from the Honorable Minister Louis Farrakhan would take us all day. That's a subject in and of itself. You know, we are going to be judged by the work that we do, and we're either going to be allowed or denied access to heaven according to our conscious behavior, based on our deeds here. You follow what I'm saying? So we need to understand that particular dynamic. But I can say I've learned

from all the Muhammad's. If it were not for Master Fard
Muhammad, we would not be sitting here, calling each other
brother and operating on the basis of trying to advance the cause of
Islam; we would not be sitting here. If it wasn't for the sacrifices
Elijah Muhammad made, we wouldn't be sitting here. If it wasn't
for the sacrifice that Elijah Muhammad's family made and all of his
ministers; Louis Farrakhan, Silis Muhammad, Warith Deen
Muhammad made, we wouldn't be sitting here. So we can't single
out one and say this one is better than the other one; I'm shunning
this one and respect that one, but I only have a small amount of
respect for that one; I don't understand what that one said. It's best
that we understand the whole family because each one of those great
men has done, is doing a great work and made a sacrifice that we
can even sit here and have this particular kind of conversation.
Plain and simple....plain and simple.

Al Mumin: You know, heard of the recent passing of Imam Warith
Deen Muhammad?

Professor Griff: Yes, but in the Black African family, we don't
revere great men as being gone, being dead. We don't speak that
kind of language. In the Black African consists of those that were,
those that are, and those that will be, so he is still here with us

Al Mumin: Yes sir, alright. More specifically, I am a follower of the
Honorable Silis Muhammad; I would want to know what you think
of him and his work? How much aware of you of his work?

Professor Griff: I'm not really aware of his work. But, I met the
brother and have a lot of great respect for him. I remember when
Minister Farrakhan brought him to speak; there was a lot of
dialogue going on. Every now and then I get the paper; I see the
brothers, I greet the brothers and have small dialogue. My think is
this, any Muslim who would advance the cause of Islam; who pricks
the consciousness of us as a people to advance our cause, we have to
give thanks and honor to. I don't know enough about Silis
Muhammad or Warith Deen Muhammad to even speak on it,
because my two brothers, in my early introduction to Islam were in

150

the Nation of Islam, headed by the Most Honorable Elijah Muhammad and now The Honorable Minister Louis Farrakhan. So that has been my introduction into Islam and the scope of my awareness. Now, I've sat with and had conversations with other people who were in Islam. I didn't get off in depth into any other school of thought, if I can use that particular language.

Al Mumin: Well, just for a little brief moment. Mr. Muhammad's major work is reparations and human rights for African descendent people, and finally exodus; having a nation we can call our own. He has dedicated his life and the rest of his life toward that cause, working with leaders of 19 different countries. So he's a known personality within the United Nations amongst these other leaders, and he's represented all Black people who are descendants of the enslaved Africans. So what do you think about reparations, the fight in the United Nations, self determination for our people; meaning the mission toward going back home and having our own nation instead of trying to make it all right here. Cause Mr. Muhammad represents that route going and leaving here just like the Honorable Elijah Muhammad put us on this course. On the back of every Muhammad speaks he would say, we want the reparations for 20 years, either on this continent or elsewhere in our own separate state; so he's going along that route. So I just wanted to know, how do you view that position versus staying in America and working our problems out over here.

Professor Griff: Well, I'm not; I can't honestly say I would agree with that, and it shouldn't be a situation where I agree or disagree. Everyone has their own methodology. I'm for reparations; I'm for repairing the damage. I'm for getting back everything that was taken from us, including the self. But when it comes to leaving America? No. We're going to take what we need here; 8 to 10 states that we can call our own, and we're going to set up something on any other continent. Because if you study your lessons, it teaches us that there's a 196,940,000 square miles of this planet. We ruled it from our throne they called Africa. Alright? But this is not their land. This is our brother, the Native Americans land. So ain't no reason why we got to pack up and leave unless the Native American says we

151

should leave. No, we want 8 to 10 states that we can call our own here, and we're going to set up dual citizenship in any other country that we choose. I'm saying we should set up dual citizenship on the continent, and we should set up dual citizenship in Brazil where a large number of our people are at. Once we do that, we will be able to take our rightful place and sit our people back on the throne where we belong. I'm not packing up going nowhere. If there's going to be a battle, there's going to be a battle inside of American and outside of America. So, this whole idea of going somewhere else? No, not an option for me. Not an option. No, I'm going to connect with my revolutionary brothers around the globe, and if we have to shut it down, then we'll shut it down; plain and simple. That's the mindset. That's the mind frame. That's what I want to pass on just in case I never do another interview another day in my life. No one understands that if I walk out and get hit by a car now, and pass on, and pass forward, I want people to know, no, we're going to stake our claim here, we want 8 to 10 states here we can call our own, we're going to set our flag in this soil here, along with setting up dual citizenship on other continents.

Al Mumin: So can I ask you a brief question concerning this one point. Because I am a believer in the Honorable Elijah Muhammad teachings, and one of his main teachings, he taught on the Mother Plane. He said that Master Fard Muhammad taught him that there's a Mother Plane, and the sole purpose of the Mother Plane was to destroy this wicked world. And the number one enemy, the United States of America, will be hit first by 1,500 baby planes and bombs that will go inside one mile and will go from north, south, east, and west; 2,000 by 3,000 square area of the United States, and none of them will be dropped on water, they will be dropped on cities, and they are time bombs. And once they blow up, I think he said, about 12 mile high flames, he said all life will be killed in the United States of America, and it will burn for 390 years and it will take another 610 years to cool off, and for 1,000 years there would be no life in the United States; this area they call the United States today and that a 1,000 years after that, there would be new vegetation and that the new world would begin. So anybody that would stay here would be destroyed. So do you believe in that teaching?

Professor Griff: Of course, but Allah is not going to destroy the true believer. So we're going to stay here and stake claim until we get that divine order. Once we get that divine order, then that's the main purpose and the reason why I said we need to set up dual citizenship. You just answered the question, because if we decide to go and we don't set up something elsewhere, where will we go?

Al Mumin: So to get clarification, you mean stay here until there's an order given that the Mother Plane has to do her work?

Professor Griff: No, I said a divine order. It has to be a divine order. But what I mean by that is we're operating in the third dimension. A third dimension paradigm; in order to get the divine order, you at least have to be in tune with the self and then activating the higher self in order to receive the instructions. Are you following me?

Al Mumin: I believe so, yes sir.

Professor Griff: So we have to be able to set up, like I said, dual citizenship on other continents so we will have some place to go. You're not just going to transport 30 to 60 million people on a weekend. Are you following me?

Al Mumin: Yes sir. So what do you think of the Obama presidency, or if Obama is elected, the fact that Barack Obama is running, that he's won the Democratic nomination, and has gotten as far as an African American get can or has gotten in history; just the whole campaign and what does it mean to our people?

Professor Griff: Well, just to answer the first part of that and just to set the record straight, I don't believe in voting. I wouldn't encourage anyone to vote. The vote is a d_mn scam, that's first of all. And then who are we to really think that in 2008 that just because a black man is running that we are going to receive justice from this government. Even if he is president, do we talk everything that Silis Muhammad taught, the Honorable Elijah Muhammad taught

Professor Griff: Minister Louis Farrakhan taught, the Most Honorable Elijah Muhammad taught, to just put it aside and not seek justice from this government? No. I think even if Barack Obama is selected President, I don't think black men and women will get justice at all. Now that may have taken care of the second part of your question, because first of all, I'm not an African American. It's sad that he believes he is.   Cause we have to understand this point and I want you to get this real clear. African Americans, African Americans cannot petition this government for reparations. Are you following me?   14 amendment citizens, you cannot petition this government and demand reparations. If you're a Black African you can. Are you following me? So we need to be very careful of the language that we use. If you are a subject of the crown, if you are a subject of the empire of the city, if you're a subject of the Vatican, London and the District of Columbia, no you're not going to get reparations, cause you're not even citizens.

Al Mumin: Are you aware of the name Afro descendants that the leaders over 19 countries were in the western Diaspora have been able to be recognized in the United Nations to represent all black descendants of enslaved Africans?

Professor Griff: And I think that's a very brilliant thing, that's very beautiful for the time being. Elijah Muhammad asked the question, "who is the original man?" and if we stick to our lessons, and that's our point of reference, none of this is confusing.

Al Mumin: Yes sir. As a follow up to what you were saying, Mr. Muhammad put out a press release called An Obama Presidency: America's Great Deception. And basically, he said Obama was just an illusion that America is using at this day and time to fool our people, especially if he does win. I know you haven't had a chance to read it.

Professor Griff: Yeah the writing is too small and I don't have my glasses.

Al Mumin: Yes sir. I thought about blowing it up bigger. I'll have to get you a better copy. But inasmuch as you have not read the press release you can't really comment....

Professor Griff: I mean we can just concentrate on that particular point if I can just use your pen. If you're saying that Silis Muhammad said Obama is an illusion alright, then we have to go back and ask ourselves the question, 'who is manufacturing and creating this illusion and then, what is the main purpose for creating the Obama illusion in order to do what? What is the whole quote?

Al Mumin: Well, I was paraphrasing. He said basically it's to fool our people, to fool Black people in America.

Professor Griff: To bring about?

Al Mumin: He calls it America's great deception. The title alone in a nutshell tells you what the press release is about.

Professor Griff: alright so if that's the case we have to see who's pulling the strings, and once we figure out who's pulling the strings, then we can find out about the agenda. If Obama is the new face for imperialism, if he's the new face for fascism, then okay, we understand, we understand what the dilemma is we understand what the main purpose of having a Black man as president. My take on it was the fact that they are trying to get back on the continent of Africa, 'cause these people cannot survive without melanin. Are you following me? We need to understand this particular dynamic, and if that's the particular dynamic, then we need to understand that how and what purpose does Barack Obama serve in the overall scheme of things. And if he's elected, or selected, then he only has four years to pull it off! So, then what plans do they have in place already that's going to create this illusion that things are getting better, and then what's going to go on behind the scenes. If you've seen the movie The Wizard of Oz, you've seen the four characters which represent four aspects of what was going on in the society at that time. And the yellow brick road symbolizing the gold, how the streets may have been paved with gold, but it led to a very tragic end, for not only the wicked witch of the west, you understand what I'm saying, but also for that little short impotent little character behind the curtain pulling the strings, you understand what I'm saying? Giving the illusion that he's a very big uhm uhm, what do you call it, as they teach in the scripture, when they talk about the snake in the Garden of Eden. If you study the scripture from an esoteric point of view you read about the snake in the scripture in Genesis, but hell by the time you get to Revelations, he's a big dragon! So we need to understand that process and how did he get to big this dragon. But the whole time it's someone real short pulling the lever and the strings behind the scene. Do you understand what I'm saying? And we need to understand that, and that's the cover that needs to be pulled, that's the curtain that needs to be pulled back in order to deal with the illusion. You understand what I'm saying? That illusion to bring about that conclusion. And you know that's not necessarily the solution. That's not going to be the solution. That's not the solution to our woes here in America and throughout the world. No, not at all. We act as though November 5th, everyone's going to get 40 acres and mule. That's not going to happen. That's not going to happen.

Al Mumin: Yes sir. So alright Professor Griff. I appreciate your time. I appreciate you granting this interview to Muhammad Speaks and Lost Found Nation of Islam under the Honorable Silis Muhammad.

Professor Griff: You mind if I just give the people my information? You can reach me at www.hdqtrz.com or www.publicenemy.com. Or you can just go up on myspace/professorgriff of public enemy or myspace/xminista. My number is 678-557-2919, and hopefully you can gain something from this very timely interview we're doing. Hopefully we can get this edited and get this out before you go behind the curtain and pull the lever to see who's going to become the next president of the United Snakes of America. Hopefully this interview will awaken the inner self so you can activate the God consciousness so we can truly do what Elijah Muhammad said which is to accept your own and be yourself. Peace, love, happiness, and As Salaam Alaikum.

Al Mumin: Wa Alaikum Salaam.

SWITZERLAND - JANUARY 01: MONTREUX ROCK FESTIVAL Photo of PUBLIC ENEMY, front L-R Flavor Flav, Chuck D, Professor Griff (Photo by Suzie Gibbons/Redferns)

THE RED PILL
THE BLACK DOT AND PROFESSOR GRIFF
FOR PBS IN MILWAUKEE by Alderman Mike McGee Jr. 2008

Interviewer: The question for Black Dot is what advice would you give young MC's looking to break into the game into the business of real or true hip hop and Griff can definitely answer that with the business format he put forth and the workshops he's going to do in Milwaukee, and he may do throughout the nation.

Black Dot: Well, the advice I would give to a young MC is to first begin to understand the power of his words, because the power of his words will determine just the effect it will have on the people. The young ones need to know that their words carry energy and vibrations to them and negative worlds will destroy things even beyond the ethers that they can physically see and positive words build things and construct things in a certain nature. So watch your words first, understand that this is a business. That's why they call it the music business, so if you don't understand the dynamics of the business aspects, then what you get is what you deserve. Understanding the inner and outer aspects of the business, study and research what has already been said and what hasn't been said, because you don't want to reinforce someone else's message. Find your path. Find your niche. And when you do that you can stand alone because they can say 'he sounds like him and she sounds like this one.' All they can say is you are who you are.

Interviewer: And then brother Griff, just going into the digital age, it's time for brothers and sisters going into the industry to stop worrying about trying to get signed.

Professor Griff: right well I think the whole idea of an artist trying to perfect their craft and trying to get into the music industry, that once upon a time we bought and sold 8 tracks. Then once upon a time we sold and bought the physical wax. Then once upon a time we bought and sold the cassette. Now there are mediums that we buy and sell through that are probably beyond what we are grasping right now. We can grasp the physical CD. It's hard for people to understand that when we get down to chips in phones, chips in I pods, chips in computer components and that kind of thing. That's going to be the medium now. The average phone now can hold two or three songs. So in a few years you're talking about the digital revolution, and when you talk about the revolution will not be televised, the revolution is going to be digitized to the point where it's going to change. And change is good when you're talking about complete conscious, constructive change. But will the average artist have enough knowledge to say 'okay I can change and adapt to the time in order to make what I'm saying and doing relevant?' Can they do that? If you're going to do that then you're basically going to have to do like Black Dot said, know, understand, and study what came before you, the words and the frequency of the words you're using now, and all those things are going to lead you to your ultimate goal that we're going to be living in.

Interviewer: And let's just talk about frequency since you brought that up. That's a question I definitely had in mind. What does frequency mean for the laymen who doesn't understand what vibration and frequency means?

Black Dot: Well, with frequency, we're talking about channels. Just like, uhm, I give this demonstration on one of my DVD's that just like when you're listening to a radio station and you want to listen to another radio station down the dial, you change the frequency, you tune into a different channel to get that particular information. Now that other station is still there, but you can no longer hear it because you've chosen to tune into a different frequency and that could be me and you being on the same frequency meaning we understand each other beyond what most people may understand. So when two brothers are on the same frequency we are moving in the same accord. We understand. We can communicate with each other not even verbally. We can communicate on other levels. It may be by the work that we're doing. Vibrations in general... or Griff do you want to answer that?

Professor Griff: Well, I want you to talk about the Ohm.

Black Dot: Oh, okay.

Professor Griff: Simply because the Ohm is the greatest sound. Everything that vibrates is in sync with the Ohm; everything that vibrates on a positive, I should say. Matter of fact, everything, be it negative or positive vibrates. Now when you talk about the Ohm, you talk about two sounds that are inside it, the "ah" and the "oh". You understand what I'm saying? Especially when we deal with the higher self and those indigenous names that the indigenous people called the higher self or God, that sound is inside the name. You got Jah, Pattah, Allah, you understand what I'm saying? The vibratory frequency is there. Uhm, and when dealing with the ohm being the larger sound, that frequency runs through everything. Now imagine a people having to save themselves or understand themselves using the language of another people; and having to constantly recreate and be co-creators with the Creator and recreate inventive ways to save ourselves, using someone else's language! So when our language was taken away from us, we have to now communicate like we use to communicate. Now when we say, 'We don't see eye to eye', and we do this (Professor Griff gestures eye to eye contact), it's not the two physical eyes, it's the pineal gland where we're trying to connect. Do you understand what I'm saying? So when you're talking about the ohm and you're talking about frequencies, he was absolutely correct. You go down the dial, the other station is still there, you just don't hear it because you're not picking it up on that particular frequency. You've changed to another frequency. Now in the music industry we deal with a higher frequency or a lower frequency. The music we're hearing today is vibrating on a lower frequency, and everything below the navel, dealing with the lower chakras, is sending that negative energy back to the higher chakra, back to the pineal gland, back to the pituitary gland, and it's affecting us because that vibratory frequency of the music, especially the bass tones, is causing you to do things that you're just unaware.

Interviewer: So let me ask this then, 'cause I think it goes in line with the questions that we've presented. Back in the day with Public Enemy, Public Enemy was on a vibration frequency that a lot of the music today is not on. They're on a whole 'nother station. So to be in tune with the people and your higher self, what MC's or artists today, if any that you can think of, are even on that level?

Professor Griff: Well, he lived it, he was there up in Boogie down, up in Harlem. He was in that grid so to speak, so he can definitely speak on that.

Black Dot: Well, in this day and time, nothing has surpassed, in my personal opinion, the vibratory frequency that Public Enemy put out. There are those who have come close to it and who are trying to use the frequency that was there to you know, tap themselves in; you have Dead Prez, Common puts out some good music; Talib Kwale, the Coup, Paris. Its brothers who are still carrying the spirit of that frequency, but Public Enemy, there will only be one. There will never be another that comes and raises the vibratory frequency the way they did. However, there are diabolical ones who understood that, and therefore, the battle begins to lower the frequency, and keep the frequency of music, sound, thought and energy vibrating on extremely low levels, and that's the war that we're fighting. People have got to stop thinking that we're just fighting a physical war. We are fighting a spiritual war. We're fighting a war of the unseen and there are those who understand who we are, and how we vibrate. Because when things move..... If I drop a quarter or a rock in the water and it starts to ripple, that ripple goes all the way throughout the ocean. So just like when you hear a group who vibrates like that and we are 70% water, so when Public Enemy came and they started to ruffle up the energy in the water of the people and it started spreading throughout the people. So understand, there are those who are trying to cut off that energy because they know how we operate.

Professor Griff: And just to add on to that, how Public Enemy got to that point, because there were artists and a vibratory frequency already out there; laid down by Grand Master Flash, Melle Mel, The Zulu Nation; did a work outside of the context of the music. When you heard of the Zulu Nation, you was like, "woo, the Zulu's? From the mother land?" You understand what I'm saying? 'Cause that was a work outside of the context of the music. Do you understand what I'm saying? I don't know how people view African Bambata and the Zulu Nation today, but if you look back you say wait, they did something that was a lot larger than we ever imagined because who was talking Black and who was calling themselves African then? Do you understand what I'm saying? To say I'm Africa, Bambata, part of the Zulu Nation? Come on man that was monumental.

THIR TEEN

VIBRATORY FREQUENCY

"From Ndoki (Non-Human) to Muntu (Human)"
Association of Black Psychologist Annual Convention July 30, 2009

In October 2008 Professor Griff of the consciousness raising rap group Public Enemy granted PsychDiscourse an exclusive interview. The interview was orchestrated by Kevin Washington, Ph.D. with the assistance of Nicole Coleman, Ph.D. These scholars engage in the process of unfolding and understanding dimensions of African/Black contemporary life with the emphasis on revealing the healing power of the African Spirit. The interview was so powerful that they have been encouraged to expand the discourse. What follows is the first part of a three part series with Professor Griff and the Healing Elements of Hip Hop.

Kevin Washington: Hello.

Professor Griff: Yes.

Kevin Washington: Griff.

Professor Griff: Yes.

Kevin Washington: Alright. Thank you for taken out your time to be with us today.

Professor Griff: Oh, that's alright.

Kevin Washington: Nicole Coleman is going to be on the line, too. So anyway, thank you, thank you for giving us a call. This is being recorded for the *Psychdiscourse*, the newsletter/news journal for the Association of Black Psychologists. This particular issue that we are talking about deals with the hip-hop movement and the psychological implications of the hip-hop movement. So I'm going to go through a series of questions and we'll just have a conversation. We will respect your time. It will be printed in the *Psychdiscourse*.

Kevin Washington: Nicole Coleman has joined us so we are going to proceed.

Nicole Coleman: Hi, Professor.

Professor Griff: Nicole, are you okay?

Nicole Coleman: Yes, I'm doing well.

Professor Griff: I'm very proud of you.

Kevin Washington: Nicole does some powerful work around hip-hop and the implications of hip-hop for Black women; so she may have some knowledge to throw in about that. First, what I want to do is I want to congratulate you on your recording project. You said that you're working on next release with 7th Octave, your musical group. Tell us a little bit about that project.

Professor Griff: Ah, yes, simply because I think when we read the history of hip-hop and all the fusions and everything that hip-hop spawned, even when we look back, you know, at those brothers and sisters that came up speaking truth to power especially during the golden era of hip-hop. I think this particular album which I entitled *God Damage* which in of itself is something to explain. Hopefully it will stand as one of those pivotal pieces that I can honestly look up to and be proud of. I borrowed the DNA from James Brown and Jimi Hendrix and infused it to present this rap/metal fusion called Heavy Mental in the Revolutionary Age of Ghetto Metal.

166

Kevin Washington: Wow, wow. Heavy mental – that sounds powerful.

Professor Griff: But it sits in a revolutionary age of ghetto metal though, we can't forget the ghetto metal. All these genres of music come from us. We need to treat it as such. We treat rock and metal and a lot of these fusions and a lot of these genres of music like stepchildren. We don't dress them well. We don't take care of them so other people adopt them and it becomes theirs.

Nicole Coleman: We give it away.

Kevin Washington: This ghetto metal – explain more about that.

Professor Griff: Well, simply because our language was taken away from us, we can't call it for what it really is in dealing with our aura and our 12 myelinated senses that we have, with our high concentration of melanin. We can't go back and call it what we really want to call it. We have to speak the English language. We have to speak to a people now that have been dumbed down to a point there's a certain aspect to the English that they would only understand. This is why we call it ghetto metal.

Nicole Coleman: That's like when Lauryn Hill says "I added a mother f_cker so you ignorant niggers hear me."

Professor Griff: Thank you, exactly. So when we bring it down to that level, hopefully, there's something in it that will raise them up, their consciousness level up.

Nicole Coleman: Right.

Kevin Washington: Alright. So now, let's deal with these basics about hip-hop. We'll get to the consciousness-raising insight. How do you define hip-hop?

Professor Griff: Well in a nutshell, to be real brief, hip-hop's definition as given to us by KRS-One, introduced to me through

Minister Server the Temple of Hip-hop is an acronym: *Higher Infinite Power Healing Our People.* So hip-hop can be summed up as a higher infinite power and this power is designed to heal our people. Under the umbrella of hip-hop, you have the four elements.

Kevin Washington: Okay. And those four elements?

Professor Griff: The four elements: those who told the stories, we get the MC. Those who wrote the hieroglyphs and left the signs and symbols for us to connect with the higher self, you get the graph writers – graffiti. Those that construct their bodies to certain movements to tell the story, of course, you get the breakdancer. On top of that, to keep the heartbeat and the rhythm of the nine systems in the body, including the other systems that we connect to, we get the heartbeat of it all which is the drum – deejay.

Kevin Washington: So you mentioned the nine systems and the twelve elements. We probably have to get that clarified. What are those nine systems that you talked about?

Professor Griff: When you talk about the nine systems of the body, you can look at any biology book and figure that out. But we have to understand that those nine systems have to be looked at metaphorically speaking when we relate them to the aspects of hip-hop. If you look at what hip-hop came from, if you can go back for just a brief second, and if we pull back from those four natural elements of the universe, we would have to base things on the natural elements of the universe. We can't just make up things as we go along. So when hip-hop was constructed and put together, yes, we have the four elements of hip-hop which I just explained but those four elements of hip-hop were tapped into earth, air, fire and water - something that we could always connect back to. These are the things that we use to elevate our consciousness in hip-hop, in a chaotic world. You really have order out of chaos. We put together an order and we structured it based on who we are and our genetical make-up. We pulled it out of the self and we presented it to the world as an art form called hip-hop – higher infinite power healing our people. So it has a healing element. Of course, it has an

168

entertainment element. It has all these elements to it and you can't just say that hip-hop is just music and entertainment. When you listen to a song and say "That's hip-hop." No, it's a lot deeper than that; a whole lot deeper than that.

Kevin Washington: That part about healing is really what we're going to pull this thing into. So those nine systems of the body and the four elements, which element of hip-hop ties into the element of water?

Professor Griff: Well, the BBoy because the BBoy has the fluid flow to his movement. Do you understand what I'm saying? We could also attribute that in some aspects to the MC because now in hip-hop, we ask the brother "Do you have a flow?" You could flow like water. Water standing still, if it's stagnant, it collects fungus and bugs and all these kinds of stuff

Kevin Washington: Right.

Professor Griff: Debris. So it has to flow. Let's keep this in mind. One of the elements, such as water, they pertain to all of the elements. If you're looking at the tree of life, if you're looking at the human body, the tree of life, when we take in water which symbolizes wisdom in hip-hop, then it affects all the other systems.

Kevin Washington: Okay, so fire?

Professor Griff: Fire would definitely represent the MC, the passion.

Kevin Washington: Okay.

Professor Griff: Dealing with the lower chakras, that passion, that fire, that energy. It's creating that energy which is symbolized in metaphysics as the kundalini energy traveling up the base of the spine and tapping the pioneer grant. A lot of times I've seen Jay-Z, I've seen Biggie go in the studio with no notes, no pen, no pad and come out with a song.

169

Kevin Washington: Going from their lower self to their higher self.

Professor Griff: Exactly, the higher consciousness.

Kevin Washington: Wow the purveyor of higher consciousness. Air – which one deals with air?

Professor Griff: Air is the deejay. Air, basically, in using a different form of alchemy. The deejay specializes in that simply because he's taking old records that our grandma had in the closet and mix it with our records that we may have bought or our sister or brother had laying around. We fused different beats from different genres of music to make hip-hop. The deejay is a master at this because he took two turntables and created this thing called the mixer and put it in between them and we put various elements together. We turned metal into gold, which is alchemy. We used a higher form of alchemy. This is what the deejay does. The deejay uses a higher form of alchemy to make you dance, to make you move. You can't just use any beat on two turntables. You had to be a scientist to know how to do that. To keep the dance floor filled? You had to be a scientist.

Kevin Washington: This speaks to the mutation of life sustaining resources. What about the earth element?

Professor Griff: The earth element is the graffiti. This earth element grounds you. This earth element will last a lot longer than any individual, as we've seen in the hieroglyphs.

Kevin Washington: Like the Metu Neter, I heard you say in one of your lectures.

Professor Griff: Exactly, simply because the Metu Neter is the divine writing of our ancestors from Kemet. Once we've etched it in stone, it metamorphoses and takes on a spirit. Our people didn't have a whole lot of time to write manuscripts upon manuscripts. This is why a picture is worth a thousand words. One hieroglyph or Metu Neter and it speaks volumes. So this is why we ground ourselves

170

with graffiti by leaving our spirit etched in stone. Not only do we leave it etched in stone, we leave it etched in the souls and in the hearts of those that participate in this thing that we call hip-hop – higher infinite power healing our people.

Kevin Washington: Then that lives forever.

Professor Griff: Exactly. The foundation has already been laid by our ancestors a long, long time ago. Even if they destroyed the physical pyramids, the physical pyramid text is written in the genetic codes of our people.

Kevin Washington: That's what coming out through hip-hop.

Professor Griff: Exactly. All you have to do is get Black people together and put on the right beat and it's on.

Kevin Washington: How did Public Enemy get started? How did you get started in hip-hop?

Professor Griff: How I got started in hip-hop back in the 1970's. I think I'm telling my age right now. I was a deejay in high school. Hip-hop wasn't even a part of what we're dealing with at that time. When hip-hop hit Long Island - we called it Strong Island, it's just something that we naturally gravitated towards. It was happening kind of like simultaneously so by the time it hit Long Island, we jumped on it. That was ten years later when Public Enemy got started. So hip-hop was already established. When Public Enemy came on the scene, we were sparked by Melle Mel's song The Message. We basically stood back and said "Wait a minute. That's what we want to do." We want to make music like that. We began our journey, stepping with our left foot forward to trample evil. We said we're going to raise the consciousness level of our people. We attempted to do that and the rest is history.

Kevin Washington: Hearing "It's like a jungle sometimes it makes me wonder how I keep from going under" had an impact on you all. So that's how Public Enemy started.

Professor Griff: Exactly, simply because the rest of that song went like this: "Don't push me because I'm close to the edge. And I'm trying not to lose my head." You understand what I'm saying? He was telling a story that all of us can identify with and we can't deny that; can't deny that at all.

Kevin Washington: Let me slide into this piece about, as you mentioned, the powerful elements of hip-hop. How has hip-hop been used to our detriment? We talked about it being used in healing. How has it been used to our detriment?

Professor Griff: Well, we can sit back and look at some of the imagery in hip-hop. Some of the imagery may sound a little like this: in the videos, you may see half-clad women. You always see stacks of hundred-dollar bills. You always see money flowing. You always see Cristal popping. You always see fogged out, animalistic behavior, posturing from the brothers always yanking on their gold and platinum-gilded chains, acquisition of wealth. These are some of the themes that permeate rap videos, if you want to just look at the imagery. If you want to look at some of the themes, we can look at "Get Rich or Die Trying," "Money, Hoes and Clothes is All A Nigger Knows." These are themes that permeate hip-hop. This is going on in a daily and consistent basis with nobody offering any opposition to these things. These brothers are left free to express themselves however they want to express themselves. If you know better, you'd do better. So we start looking at information that came out by John Logan who's a Ph.D. He wrote *The Rap, Ritual, and Reality,* violent music makes violent kids. We have to look at the reality of that. That's true.

Nicole Coleman: Can you talk a little bit about the industry side – how much of that is intentionally perpetuated? If we leave them unattended without guidance, we'll continue to speak about these things. I wonder how much of that is pushed by the industry and the capitalism involved in the industry?

Professor Griff: What we need to understand is there's a psychological war going on but it's going on a covert level. They

172

themselves said that if you capture their minds and their hearts, their souls will follow. They believe that the people living in this particular state, as they call it, will basically all they have to do is put a system among us and the culture would erode itself. They wrote these things. If you study the Tavistock Institute of Technology, they wrote these things about our people and we have to understand this particular dynamic. There was a book that I was studying The Tavistock Institute of Human Relations Shaping the Moral, Spiritual, Cultural, Political and Economic Decline of the United States of America. They admitted themselves that they would devise and develop twelve tones jointly with British intelligence operatives operating here in America. If you look up Operation Paper Clip, it will give you an idea as to who these people are. They were these doctors and engineers that were brought to America secretly. They didn't leave out hip-hop. They developed these tones and these tones were put among us to erode the morals of the listener. We would take these tones, use these tones and we would degrade ourselves. That's exactly what happened shortly after that, in a book entitled The First Limited Edition of The American Directory of Certified: Uncle Toms on page 236, it talks about the nefarious negrotization of rap music. BET came along, along with Quincy Jones's Vibe magazine that end up using these tones, using these themes and using this particular imagery to dumb down hip-hop, thus dumbing down black people. The first group that came out of that particular experiment was NWA. They said these things themselves. Also in a book by William Cooper - do you remember William Cooper who wrote Behold the Pale Horse?

Kevin Washington: Yes.

Nicole Coleman: Right.

Professor Griff: They ended up shooting William Cooper in the head. William Cooper, in his book Behold the Pale Horse a former naval officer in regards to your document concerning the American public. Diversion, he says, is the primary strategy. The simplest method of regaining control of the public is to keep the public undisciplined and ignorant of basic system principles while keeping

173

them confused, disorganized, distracted with matters of no real importance. Whereas the media keeps the adult population's attention diverted from the real social issues and captivated by matters of no real importance, the schools keep the young public ignorant of real mathematics, real economics, real law, and real history. Entertainment is kept below the sixth grade level. The public is kept busy working and the result is no time to think. That's exactly what we're going through now. Hip-hop went from the first ten years when it laid the base to the next ten years after that – the golden era of hip-hop. After that, we got gangsta rap. Then we went through the all-out-of-control phase and the fogged-out phase. Now, we're at the pimping stage of it. This is the way hip-hop is. The next phase is going to be brothers coming on stage wearing skirts, lipsticks and earrings and it's going to be over after that.

Nicole Coleman: That's interesting. So I get a focus group of young black women asking them about their perceptions of images of hip-hop and how they think it influences them personally and how they think it influences how other people see us as black women as a group. One of the participants in the group said "It really just depends on what sells." She said, "If they start selling cartoons in the video is what sells, then you'll see everybody having cartoons in their videos." There's no end to the level of ridiculousness that we will see it go to if it is what quells the masses, or what serves to continue to reinforce the foolishness that exists out there.

Kevin Washington: Right.

Professor Griff: And I think that's real because we have real life examples of what you're talking about. Do you remember when the movie Scarface came out?

Kevin Washington: Right?

Professor Griff: Scarface is probably one of the most detrimental films to the black psyche simply because it spawned a whole heap of things. It gave instructions on how to sell drugs. It gave instructions and a code to the street. It made black rappers take on gangster names like Lucky Luciano and Bugsy Siegel, Pretty Boy Floyd and Babyface Nelson. A lot of these guys were Jewish mafia gangsters but you turn around and you see rappers with these names. This was a psychological covert war that was put among us. It's called Operation Hollywood, you know what I'm saying? These magazines have the nerve to turn around and ask the question in their source magazine "Hip-hop Behind Bars: An In-depth Look at America's Criminal Justice System, Are We the Targets?" Some of the brothers on the cover had names like C Murder, Billy Siegel. Do you understand what I'm saying? All we did was borrow that energy and that frequency and we became it. Like produces like.

Kevin Washington: Right.

Professor Griff: You want to keep Tupac only talk about murder? That's how he met his end. Biggie always talked about death: life after death and all these themes that Biggie came with. You know between his albums Going Out and Coming In, he left us. That same energy.

Kevin Washington: So you use this idea of ministry with hip-hop. Hip-hop is a type of ministry. Is that what you're trying to tell us?

Professor Griff: Not trying to tell you. I gave you that example in the last twenty years being the Minister of Information that Chuck D called rap the CNN of the black community. This is how we were informed. We were always informed in most cases by the poets, by the culture, by the songs. Aretha Franklin warned us. Am I right or wrong? James Brown told a story. Marvin Gaye. We can quote his soul music all day long. In most cases, this is how we got our information. Staples Singers said it. Al Green said it. Temptations said it, if you can remember.

Kevin Washington: That's right. So the idea that I was going to get into is this covert attack on hip-hop and going to this question: since we see how, as you said, it's used to our detriment, can you speak more about how we can use hip-hop for our good? And then what are some next steps for hip-hop?

Professor Griff: Well like the symbol of Sankofa bird teaches us. You see the Sankofa bird moving forward with its left foot trampling evil. But in order to move forward, the first step forward is to go back. We have to understand what our black African ancestors why they left us this symbol. We have to understand why J. Edgar Hoover orchestrated and put together the counter-intelligence program and what was the main objective. I think we all know, especially those on the phone, the main objective was to prevent the rise of the black Messiah. This energy, the people that came after J. Edgar Hoover don't understand that that messianic voice, they heard it in hip-hop. They heard it in the frequency of the music. They heard it in the drum and then they really heard it when Public Enemy stepped on the scene and spawned and gave birth to other groups like Brand Nubian, Poor Righteous Teachers, KRS-One, Wise Intelligent and a lot of other brothers and sisters that step forth. So it gave birth to this and it was uncontrollable simply because it posed a problem for white people, simply because Johnnie, Suzie, Amy, Jennifer, Greg and the rest of them had posters of NWA and Public Enemy on their walls. Who is this Chuck D guy? Who's KRS-One? Who's the Brand Nubian? The kids can understand and relate to it but parents weren't having it. Then it became a problem. When we started seeing Public Enemy logo tattooed in the head of young white Americans, oh that posed a problem. That spoke volumes because they wanted to put together a system that they can pass on to their children. If hip-hop was interrupting that frequency, something had to be done. So now, multinational corporations own hip-hop. We have rappers like Jay-Z and Kanye West taking their oath to the Illuminati. We have to understand this particular dynamic. You see Damon Dash, Suge Knight, Irv Gotti and Jay Prince that owned labels at one time wanted to put out black people's music uncut. White people were not going for it because they had to be the gatekeepers. So these gentlemen were paid off and a lot of times, they became the gatekeepers and no material was put out for a long, long time until the invention of YouTube and Google Video. Now brothers are shooting their own videos and putting them up. Once again, it's posing a threat. They had to counteract it by establishing networks like VH1, Video Hits One which is a video station/network that never plays videos. We understand the psychological covert war that

176

they're waging. So they pay someone like Flava. They snap someone like him out of the most socially-conscious hip-hop group ever and use him to dumb hip-hop down. It probably nailed the coffin to hip-hop. That's exactly what's been done. They said "Look, we're going to take the best group that's ever made politically conscious music. Take one of members and use it to put the nail in the coffin of hip-hop." We fell for it hook, line and sinker. Now young people coming to view conscious hip-hop, they got to view it through Flava's Flavor of Love and VH1. Not good.

Nicole Coleman: Not good at all.

Kevin Washington: So the next step is taking control of it. You talked about the Vote or Die with the previous election and hip-hop being involved in that. What's happened with the Barack Obama factor and hip-hop? What's hip-hop doing with that and for that?

Professor Griff: To put a cap on that last piece, in offering a solution as we go along. We need to stand on the shoulders of all those that came before us. We need to unravel that madness. Amos Wilson wrote two beautiful works: Black on Black Violence: The Psychodynamics of Black Self-Annihilation in Service to White Domination, and his other work, The Falsification of African Consciousness. If only we stood on Amos Wilson's work, we can unravel this madness and offer some kind of solution to those Negroes that have been paid to be the spokespeople for hip-hop: Cornell West and Michael Eric Dyson. They never rubbed elbows with me at no hip-hop concert. How now in 2008 that they became the spokesmen for hip-hop? They're trying to intellectualize this thing. Only one aspect of this can be intellectualized. The rest of it is grinding in the street. Speaking about Barack Obama how we can update and remix this thing, I don't know. How to steal an election is a real dynamic that we need to put on the table. How to steal an election is what real gangsters do, not these corny studio gangsters in hip-hop. Real gangsters steal elections. Real gangsters destabilize governments. Are you following me? Real gangsters select the president. No one came to the hood to teach us the voting process.

Are you following me? So that whole process we're unaware off. We don't know that the Electoral College elects the president? We do. Then there are some things that I had put together that I know McCain, Palin, Biden or Obama won't deal with. They won't deal with the fact that the IRS is not a US government agency. They won't deal with the IMF is an agency of the UN. They won't deal with that the US has not had a Treasury Dept. since 1921 and that the Treasury Dept. is now the IMF International Monetary Fund. That the FCC, CIA, FBI, NSA and all the other alphabet gangs were never part of the United States government, including the d_mn Post Office. These people are not dealing with these things. We're blindly going to the polls voting for Barack Obama, not knowing that he's part of the blue-bloods. We need to understand this. Someone needs to educate. They purposely dumbed down when we came to this part of history. The once-powerful genre called hip-hop is no longer the voice of the voiceless. It's about money, hoes and clothes all a nigger knows. Get down and lay down. Get rich or die trying; the criminal pursuit of wealth. That's the theme they put among us and that's what we do.

Kevin Washington: I said it was going to be respect your time so we are going to rap this first of hopefully many more sessions. It's not even a close because we never close out but is there anything you want to say to our organization in this particular issue of hip-hop?

Professor Griff: I think I would have to say, as I always say, about revolution and about violence. Revolution is complete, constructive, cosmic change. Revolution is not an event; it's a process. Those that make a peaceful revolution impossible make violent revolution inevitable. Violence is not good or evil; violence is necessary. If I pass today or if I pass tomorrow, hopefully to the ancestral realm, I want people to know just that. We need to get free by any and all means necessary.

Nicole Coleman: You need to say that again, Professor Griff.

Professor Griff: I said we need to get free by any and all means necessary. I really appreciate you all.

178

Nicole Coleman: We appreciate you.

Kevin Washington: I hope that you know that we thank for pulling away from your 7th Octave project at this trying time in your life. I don't know if mind our community knowing that recently you lost your house and many of your possessions due to a house fire but I'm putting it out there that you're going through a transitional process now.

Professor Griff: Yes.

Kevin Washington: We continually give you support as you've supported us. I'm going to look at somehow ABPsi can actually support Professor Griff in his transitional process.

Professor Griff: Oh, good. Thanks. Hopefully these words, once they're transcribed down, people can read them and say "Okay, even at this brother's worst time in his life, he's still doing the work." I don't want to be patted on the back or given medals for it. I want to serve as an example of what all of us should be doing.

Nicole Coleman: Right.

Kevin Washington: Thank you, thank you Brother Griff. Anything else, Nicole, that you want to get in, if it's possible?

Nicole Coleman: No. I would like to reiterate that I hope this is a beginning conversation and I think there's a lot of opportunity for collaboration and alliance between us and how we see things on the "psychological side" and what you're talking about "hip-hop side." I think there's a lot more overlap than we may allow ourselves to have. Hopefully, we can keep moving forward in parallel doing the same work.

Professor Griff: Oh, I really appreciate you Dr. Nicole Coleman. Thanks Brother Dr. Kevin Washington. Give thanks and take care.

Nicole Coleman: Take care. Peace.

Professor Griff: Alright. Peace.

CHAPTER THIRTEEN

The Northerner

Professor Griff speaks to hip-hop our minds
"Public Enemy" member speaks at NKU

Professor Griff began his presentation on Feb. 19, in the Otto Budig Theatre by giving out his cell phone number and inviting anyone in the audience to call him for further discourse.

His mission is to raise awareness and bring the human family back together. The Minister of Information, Griff's Public Enemy moniker, invites debate, dialogue, and doesn't fear the occasional diatribe.

"I can guarantee you will not agree with everything I have to say here tonight," explains Griff, "but we have to talk. We have to have dialogue."

The Professor presses the audience to ask themselves three fundamental questions: who am I, where am I, and am I all that I ought to be?

Hip-hop stands for, "high infinite power healing our people." This is contrast to the rap sometimes mistaken for hip-hop. Hip-hop is the umbrella and rap is inside it explained Griff. Most rap contains misogynistic material within its lyrics while hip-hop is positive, uplifting and attempts to raise consciousness. This was the crusade of "Public Enemy."

"The frequency of hip-hop and with the medium of hip-hop -we wanted to bring about hip-hop mind revolution," Griff said. This revolution requires a complete, constructive, conscious change. To evolve and move forward, the masses must be educated, recognize their higher self, and progress the dissemination of information. Professor Griff emphasizes the "know-one-teach-one" philosophy.

"If you leave here with one iota of truth it is your duty and responsibility to pass it on," Griff said. "Pass something positive on to the next person."

The importance of raising awareness, educating people, easily segues into his differential between hip-hop and rap.

Some popular rap artists dumb down hip-hop. They promote a lifestyle of a jail culture. Gangster rap markets materialism, misogyny, and violence. Griff states the rap group NWA as the template. In 1991, Public Enemy was candidly telling us that project is just another word for experiment. Fast-forward eighteen years, Lil' Wayne is singing, "Lick it like a lollipop."

According to Professor Griff, the poisoning of hip-hop doesn't lie with just the record labels and marketing companies but the frequency within the music itself. "We have seven chakras in our bodies. Hip-hop stimulates those chakras and vibrates the crown chakra with its particular frequency. The low bass frequency of some popular rap music stimulates only the lower regions," Griff states. These lower chakras regions stimulate appetite and sex according to Griff. Hip-hop is a pathway of positivity, encourages expression, and isn't esoteric. "It is a bridge from the past to present," Griff states. That bridge proved successful to those in attendance.

"I have a better understanding of where I come and why I identify with the hip-hop culture. If people internalized it the world would be a better place," says **NKU** student Janol Vinson says. "It is not what the mainstream has twisted into the culture of death as **Griff** describes it."

SEIU Rally for Universal Healthcare featuring Chuck
D, Public Enemy 2008

The Evolution
YouTubeRadio.Net
Terry Kelly

TK: First and foremost Griff, I want you to explain to me why is it you chose to give to me the opportunity to provide the world with this insight and this interview when others of your caliber would easily either not be available or choose to decline? Why is it you choose to take your personal time and energy to bless us with this opportunity?

PG: First of all let me thank for you granting me with your presence and blessing me with your presence simply because you had to think enough of me, even call me to build, to share, to reason so we can put this down and etch it in stone so to speak so we can pass this on. Simply because someone else will hear this interview that we probably don't even know and we don't know how it is going to affect their lives, do understand what I am saying? And that is probably the main reason the information is coming through me as Delbert Blair teaches us, we are not our bodies. We are in our bodies, so I think it is mandatory I take heed. From what the Honorable Elijah Muhammad teaches us that we are vessels and we have to keep this temple of God clean so that particular information comes through us, untainted, you understand what I am saying, so I can pass this information on to someone else because, simply, this is not ours. We are held with the duty and responsible on a spiritual level to pass this information, to have this information come through us

186

at this juncture in the road. So, I want to galvanize the spirit of the Ancestors and call them among us to guide our deeds and guide our words for these few minutes we are going to be here together. All of the Ancestors and knowing that on a deeper level our Ancestors are in us, speaking to us. Our Ancestors speak to us from within us. It ain't nothing spooky about the Ancestor worship, you understand what I am saying? Know and understand that it is guided by a Divine force, which we will get into a little bit later on. So, I want you to hear Marcus Garvey in this interview, I want you to hear the Most Honorable Elijah Muhammad, Nobel Ali, Che' Guevara, all those that died in the middle passage and those that fought the beast. I want you to hear Steve Biko, Winnie Mandela, the Mau-Mau, we are the Moroons, I want you to hear all of the coming through us, but we have to keep the vessel clean. I may not have this opportunity to cross paths with you. This will probably happen once or twice in a lifetime. You understand what I am saying? What comes out of this particular energy with the brother sitting around this table may never happen again. You understand what I am saying? So we want people to hear this interview and grasp the principles that we are trying to lay down and extract from this those necessary lessons that they need to continue soldiering.

TK: Absolutely. In our previous phone conversation I described to you an interview I most recently did with KRS1 and during that lecture that I attended he had mentioned the word "nigger" and how he felt it was okay for white folks to use the word "nigger" and he would also encourage them to use that word more often What would be your views; one towards "nigger" and also towards the idea of people of the Caucasian race using that word casually, more often and encouraging them to do so more often?

PG: Well, not to talk about KRS1 or anyone of these particular brothers whom you know and everyone sitting around this table love them for the work that they have done. You understand what I am saying? But we have to correct these things as we see them and as we experience them. I purposely bought my laptop so I could just give you an

187

example of why it's necessary for us to check that, you understand what I am saying? I am sure; we can agree we don't control the image of Hip Hop. We don't control the image of what goes out across the globe because we don't have the means to control image. What this particular picture here is showing you is a baby sucking on a breast controlled by multi-national corporations and what they want to do is brand your child from this age. From the time that you reach maturity. Do you understand what I am saying? So multi-national corporations are coming in on this particular level so by the time it reaches the stage KRS1 was talking about, it's almost a wrap because these are the billboards that set up in the black community. Now, this is the united colors of Benetton and if you see the images of how they demonize black people, you understand what I am saying, we have to know and understand these actual demons that are controlling these images, especially with Hip Hop we have to understand this particular thing and these people are coming after us on a subconscious level. This one right here says "Multiply, computing performance and maximize the power of your employees." Where it shows brothers kneeling down, and bowing down, to this particular Caucasian gentleman coming out of a stable like they are animals. Do you understand what I am saying? So we have to understand this. This one is deep, because it says "Food for Life" but this brother is standing here with his hand cut off with a spoon attached to it. He can't even feed himself. Are you following me? Talk Benetton, United Colors of Benetton, talk about food for life. You mean to tell me you go into the Continent, cripple our people, and then you turn around and you attach a spoon so he can feed himself? When they control the food and the natural resources of the indigenous people? You understand what I am saying? So, when you talk about Play station portable white is coming? Oh, this is to let you know they are already here. Getting down to what KRS1 was talking about; Nike actually branded this particular brand called the "Nigger" brand. They said "You rappers, you want white people to call you "niggers," good, we are going to make a brand called

"Nigga Brand," we are going to put a swoosh on it and make tee shirts and sneakers and you niggers want to call yourselves niggers all day, go ahead, wear our brand. Are you following me? This speaks directly to what KRS1 was saying and talking about, and this is sad that we had to get to this particular level. Are you following me? So, for him to say and grant these people permission, when I had that phone conversation with you the other day and you told me that, that is just a license for us to go ahead and kick their ass, you understand what I am saying? And that is not going to happen, not going to happen. That may happen with a few, but, I think instinctively those people know the historical significance of us having to defend ourselves, number one from being called "boy," and we had to grow to a level where we did not want to be called no "nigger." We are the Gods, we are the Gods, and you understand what I am saying? And they know that, instinctively, they know that.

TK: Indeed. (Laughter). Alright, J. Edgar Hoover. The counter-intelligence program. In the counter-intelligence program it talks about discrediting the black man.

PG: Right.

TK: So anybody that rises up to a certain degree of information where they are able to feed knowledge to the people, the objective would be to discredit him first and by doing so taking the opportunity for people to place their faith in that person out of the equation. What are your views towards the counter intelligence program and the idea of discrediting the black man?

PG: Well, I think first of all we need to look at it from an historical perspective. J. Edgar Hoover and the counter intelligence program-cointelpro-did he not say that the main objective was to prevent the rise of a black Messiah?

TK: That's right.

PG: So, I need to ask the brothers around this table a question then, just kind of off the cuff, if he said that and it is etched in stone and it is written, he did say that, what did J. Edgar Hoover know about a black Messiah coming from us as a people that we didn't know? He even listed names and

189

organizations. He mentioned the Most Honorable Elijah Muhammad, a black liberation organization and the Black Liberation Army, Kwame Torre and other people. Dr. King and other people. So what did J. Edgar Hoover know that we have failed to get a grasp on? You understand what I am saying? So, we have to understand that particular dynamic and a Messiah comes to do what? That is the question we need to be asking ourselves? So, if the Messiah is suppose to come and deliver our people, then what did J. Edgar Hoover know in his secret files that we didn't know? Do you understand what I am saying? And then, did he have an idea of who this Messiah was going to be, where he was suppose to come from, not outside the country but come from with inside of the people. Do you understand? Because he didn't look in other places, he looked in the Hood. Do you understand what I am saying? So, J. Edgar Hover, the FBI, or the Cointelpro knew something that we didn't know. This is why he went in and he began his campaign discrediting leaders, breaking up the organizations, putting in plants and imps inside of the ranks. Not only of the Nation of Islam, but the Black Liberation Organization, Black Panther Party and this kind of thing. If they didn't kill you off and they didn't break up your party and jail the leaders, they paid them off. So, wait a minute, we see that same thing going on today. Did he not pay off Flava Flav and give him a reality show? Did he not pay off Chuck and have him on FOX news working for Air America? We don't even hear from KRS1, Chuck and all of these other people. Not to discredit them, I'm just saying on the level we should hear from them speaking truth to power. It's cool, don't get me wrong, it is nothing wrong with us doing business and go speak at the universities, getting 5, 10 thousand a pop, but what about us? How about Tay-Tay, Man-Man, Re-Re and Peanut and them and Twan in the Hood? They never get the benefit of hearing a conversation like this. Or to shakes Chuck's hand in the hood. So, I told the universities this, "Fine, so you pay me a few dollars to come in, but what you need to do is every speaker after me, or starting with me, if you bring them in on a Friday, make their _ss stay Saturday morning and go into the Hood." You understand what I am saying? Speak to them. I don't give a d_mn if it is on the street corner, the youth center, or wherever you know what I mean, it don't make a difference. Young people need to know. Re-Re and them, Man-Man, Day-Day in the Hood? They need to know,

TK: Absolutely.

PG: So we need to look into what J. Edgar Hoover was saying and why he thought a black Messiah was coming from us. It is political, but see how he turned it into a spiritual, religious thing? A Messiah's coming. That's critical. We can take J. Edgar Hoovers word and go into scriptures and figure out who the Messiah was. But that is another conversation.

TK: Going back a little bit, I want to get into the history of Public Enemy, and also more specifically, your relationship with Flava Flav during the course of your experiences with Public Enemy. In one of your previous lectures that I attended in Philadelphia, you often talked about how there would be feuding? Sometimes even fist fights between you and Flav and arguments and different things. Let's get into the nature of the experiences, how you came in and how you went out of the group and how that may have affected you personally and some of the specifics behind it?

PG: I am going to pull up a few things that's going to answer and speak to that directly. But let me just say this to sum up and give something like a backdrop of the bases. I am not going to speak long. Here we have a book in front of us. It is called The United Independent Compensatory Code System and Concept by Neale Fuller Jr. and he says, "If you do not understand racism what it is and how it works everything else you think you understand will only confuse you." And we need to understand the basis to that. Now this brother came and he laid out some "showoffs" -which I don't get a chance to even introduce when I do lectures- and there are 9 areas of "People Activity" which we are going to go over in a second, but he talks about "showing off" and we may look at this as a childish kind thing but none the less it is laid out as a basis to understand our particular behavior patterns. Now, no one in this room has this particular hairstyle that we see in the Hood now. You see the brothers with the little Mohawks? Where is this coming from?

TK: America's Top Model.

PG: Thank you. Some white faggots done put this among our people. Because we know and understand that when you are following someone walking behind them eyes are made to focus in on points. Back in the day we use to wear the hairstyle that came to a "V" and the "V" represented the crotch, the womb and we are drawn to that. You understand what I am saying? But what is with the Mohawk now? They are not praising and giving credit to the warriors among the Native American community, because they destroyed them, do you understand? So what is with this now and how does it tie in with the feminization of the African male. So, we need to look into that. Before, it was the white tee. We can go do trends that were put among us. A minute ago, it was the sagging pants, which is criminal jail culture married onto Hip Hop culture. Do you understand what I am saying? So we need to understand these trends that were put among us. Put among us for what though? A minute ago, and I see you brothers got the military stuff on. We were bombarded with this thing. What were they trying to do? Put us in military uniform to justify shooting us down in the street? Or are they sending a signal that we need to lock up regardless of who we are? To get into a military structure, you understand what I am saying and to become more militant. But I've seen cats wearing the military uniform that weren't militant. They were using it as a fashion statement until brothers like us put Marcus Garvey on a slate, or the Lion of Judah, or Haile Salassie, you understand what I am saying, and then it changed the complexion of things and then we start confronting some of the brothers. Okay, like why are you wearing this? Who is Haile Selassie? What is the Lion of Judah? Who is Marcus Garvey and these brothers couldn't answer that. So, that fashion thing died out real quick because we checked it. I told somebody this morning in a phone conversation; I said "Let me tell you something, if it wasn't for conscious people, we would have been back in slavery." "We ain't got nothing to do with slavery." "Yes, we do, we may be 100 years up from slavery, but we still suffer from slavery, the psychological effects of slavery." "Well, how can you prove that Professor Griff?" "Whose name do you have? Whose clothes do you wear? Whose food do you eat? And as Amos Wilson teaches us the last question and most important question what God do you pray to?" Where is all the ancient African spiritual concepts and systems we had put in place before they came and bought us here? You don't study Ifa. You don't study the Voudun; you understand what I am saying? You don't study Yoruba. You don't study many African principles, systems and concepts we had put in place. Even the way we study Islam is not the way we studied it then, before we introduced it as a religion to the white Arab, you understand what I am saying? We have to understand this particular....so, Francis Cress-Welsing came, and her book, "The Isis Papers: The Keys to the Colors" and said "No racism is a local and global power and dynamic structured and maintained by persons who classify themselves as white whether consciously, or subconsciously determined." Which consist of patterns of perception, logic, symbol formation, thought, speech, action and emotional response as conducted simultaneously in all areas of people activity. And those areas are economics, education, entertainment, labor law, politics, religion, sex and more for the ultimate purpose of white genetic survival and to prevent white genetic annihilation on the planet earth. So, in a nut shell, what she is saying is that genetic material that lies in the testicles of the black man can successfully annihilate white people. Now, on a conscious level do they understand this, probably not, on a subconscious level do they feel this and participate in it, yes? You understand what I am saying? So, if we laid this as a backdrop, we can honestly say this operates in all areas. Now, you think this dude know, Usher, do you think he knows why we subconsciously grab our testicles like the rappers use to do back in the day? Uh, uh. Subconsciously, those other people know. Because Dr. King says all we have to do is love them and Malcolm X came behind them and they accused him of hate. They said we need to spread love. Who made that song, "Spread love, da da, and da?"

TK: After 7, Take 6 one of those.

PG: They're afraid of that. If we just spread love oh, we would cover the whole race of them in a minute. It would be about 10 years and everybody would be brown. If every brother went out and just got 10 of them. You understand what I am saying? On a subconscious level they fear that man. So, subsequently, nobody's complexion can get through. They are barely letting brothers through my complexion and now your top models, and your top producers and all these people are light skinned people. But not only the fact that are they light skinned, they are not teaching anything like this.

TK: Right.

PG: So, they allow you to pass so they set up a buffer. And who does the buffer consist of. The metrosexual. You allow homosexual in, you allow certain things to get past, but the strong warrior brothers, no we ain't getting through. We are not getting through at all and anybody that sounds like this...this is why you see this watered down milk toast kind of interviews people like KRS1 and these other people give. Do you understand what I am saying? So speaking directly to this Flava Flav thing, which we definitely need to deal with it simply because as Brother Jahi Muhammad will tell you, I get asked that question all the time when I do lectures. "What's up with your man Flava Flav?" But, I want to speak to that directly from an esoteric point of view so people can understand it. Because a lot of times people think we beat up on people like Flava. We not doing that. But, what you are doing on TV in front of 7.5 million viewers affects us. You understand what I am saying? So I want to deal with it from a perspective where the average person listening to this and not seeing this would understand. When Public Enemy came into birth there was already 10 years of the Hip Hop oral tradition which wasn't written about until recently. In order for you to participate in Hip-Hop, you had to be there. So, when we came about, we came about a Hip-Hop mind revolution. KRS1, through his minister, Minister

Server says Hip-Hop is an acronym High Infinite Power Healing Our People and Public Enemy came about to bring about a mind revolution. So, inside the term revolution, you see the word re: meaning to go back, to bind back to and inside the word revolution if you look closer you see evolution. So, in order to evolve, we have to go back to connect ourselves to those four fundamental elements of Hip-Hop which is based on the four fundamental forces of the universe, Earth, Air, Fire and Water. See, Earth, Wind and Fire put it down, but nobody paid attention. You understand what I am saying? Revolution means complete, constructive, conscious, cosmic change. Did we do that? So, we had to bind ourselves back to the Black Panther Party, back to black revolutionary black organizations; Nation of Islam, and we had to take on a physical look to remind people, like Sista Soulja said "We are at war." Do you understand what I am saying? So, pushing forward to the Flava Flav thing. This right here, of course it gave birth to all these other brothers that you see coming up out of the 5 Percent Nation of Gods and Earths, but we don't have time to deal with that now. So, speaking directly of the Flava Flav thing speaking from a metaphysical perspective it was told to me by Jason Orr who puts on the Funk Jazz that this strong male image right here went out across the globe. When we started interpreting what the target meant the black man is sitting behind the target and we have always been a target. When you start dealing with a Flava Flav thing and the reason they came to pay him off, the opposite of what they did to a Professor Griff, destroy me, but pay a Flava Flav off. Silence Chuck and then create and pay off a group like NWA to neutralize Public Enemy. Do you understand what I am saying? So, it got deeper. Flava Flav is actually one of the first ones to have one of these reality show kind of things, but look what they did to it. They had him on a couple of talk shows and they wheeled him out in a baby carriage in a crib. We subtly use the term 'I want you come over to my crib' let's build', Frances Cress-Wessling deals with that in her chapter "The Motherf_cker and the Original Motherf_cker," I'm not making this up. But when you look at this image that goes across the globe of a grown black man coming out of a baby crib with a school clock on and horns what signal does that send out to our people across the globe? I put here "The Niggerization of Hip" America loves niggers, and hates black people. You understand what I am saying? We have to understand this particular dynamic so inside the reality show, Strange Love which stared Flava Flav and Bridget Nielson. She called him "Foofie foofie." That is the name you give to a dog or pet. He called her Gita, so Jason Orr told me to look in the book of ancient deities and we can look up Gita, or Bridgette which was her name it says: Brigette, Deity of Cemeteries, Goddess of the Dead, female counterpart of to Gita which is the name that Flava called her. So, I looked up Gita and it says: Gita, God of Dead. Gita is likely of African origin and is associated with Baron Samadhi. Children are protected by him. Gita has healing powers. He is shown as a black man wearing a coat, top hat, dark glasses and carries a cane and is usually shown with a cigar or cigarette. His sign is a square cross on a low tomb. So, I looked up the Source magazine which had Flava on the cover and the article was called "The Resurrection of the Jester King." Let's stop for a minute and go back to what J. Edgar Hoover said "...the rise of a black Messiah." Alright, "The Resurrection of the Jester King." So I scrolled down in the Source magazine and it has this "...in Haiti, those possessed by the Voodoo God of the Dead, Gita makes jokes, dresses in a dark hat, wears glasses and makes noises like kee, kee, kee, kee laughter." Is that not Flava Flav? Are you following me? So, Flava is walking around with that African Asian deity trapped in him trying to get out. But, is it for to denigrate and disgrace our people on VH1, Video hits one? No, he is supposed to be teaching some valuable lessons. But, if we pay him off and keep him on a foolish level, on a low vibration, keeps him away from the people in the Hood this information would never get to us. It would never affect his children's children. Because, now it is his duty and responsibility to pass this on. You understand what I am saying?

TK: Absolutely.

PG: So this is why you had to destroy Griff who was the Minister of Information, and pay Flava Flav off and keep Chuck quiet. I don't mean to be so long with these answers but...

TK: Please, this is perfect. (Laughter). This is perfect. This is more than I could have possibly expected and I am thankful for every moment of it. We are talking about the destruction of Professor Griff versus the perpetuation of Flava Flav and the promotion of what Flava is doing. Last night, I did a little bit of research before I came out today and I came across on YouTube some interviews you did and also some footage in relation to the fire that took place in your home and one of the things I discovered that I did not know it was mentioned that there was gas trucks already on the scene before the fire took place.

PG: No, no no that is not true. They were there the next day, but they were in abundance to a point where they flagged everyone's house on the block and then to make a long story short and a short story shorter and they came up, in documents, saying the particular house I was purchasing wasn't retrofitted to receive that much gas pressure. I don't know how long you'll brothers have been here, but they had dug up the Westend, about four or five years ago. They had torn up the street in front of Soul Veg right on into the historical Westend.

TK: It wasn't that long ago. About two years ago.

PG: Phil Valentine reported that they had put new pipes that opened and closed so they could control how much pressure and how much gas goes into those particular areas. Now you know, these so called Hoods are being retrofitted for the New World Order, meaning when they want to lock down a grid for example, I live in the 30303 zip code, now we all know if we study New World Order quote unquote Conspiracy. You know they are going to lock us down by our number. What number Griff? By your address. I live at 211 Peachtree Street, or your social security number. Right? Or your zip code. Okay, so what does that mean? If we want to lock down the 30303 grid, we control the gas, the light, the food everything that goes into that grid and we lock it and shut it down. So, if 20 revolutionaries are locked in that particular grid, they can hone in on that particular grid, pull it up on the screen, lock it down. Now, what movie came out with this information? You better put that on pause, it may take you all a minute. It was a movie with Samuel L. Jackson in it recently. Within in the last year. What they wanted to do was get the zip code to everyone's cell phone number to create a grid to find this particular fugitive.

TK: I didn't see that movie.

PG: You seen Batman?

TK: The newest Batman?

PG: With Samuel L. Jackson in it?

TK: I don't think I've seen that yet.

PG: Oh, you have got to get that movie. They went to an underground bunker where they had all the grids up on a screen. They said, "Oh we can easily find him all we have to do is send out the necessary people with cell phones, and we link the cell phones to one another creating a grid and we just track him down." You understand what I am saying? Now, why can't they just do that to one particular square mile of any one black community and lock it down and cut off the gas. Alright, how about not cut off the gas, how about we pump more gas into that particular grid and blow some houses up? A youth center, you understand what I am saying? The Mosque. Oh, we can go deeper than that.

TK: Or Professor Griff's house?

PG: Exactly, so when you look at me coming into town, because I wasn't here when that happened, trying to track down the technician that tried to turn the gas on he ended up in the hospital shortly after that. They took him out of the hospital and he is nowhere to be found. Don't know his name or what **he looks like.**

TK: Whew!

PG: I don't want anybody running up on me telling me that you are just kind of paranoid and how do you know it is a conspiracy? And, how come the brother won't step forth and tell me who he is? You understand what I am saying?

198

And as Jahi will tell you what I am saying, I haven't told my story yet. Truly, I haven't told my story yet.

TK: Word up. Alright, let's get into some of our today's lecturers such as Jill Puprum, Bobby Emmett, Phil Valentine, and Delbert Blair. Some of these names that I've mentioned I would like to know what your perspective is on the elders that are doing lectures today. Areas also where you feel may need improvement. Areas that you feel as though are highlights. Let's get into some of the lecturers who stand out in your mind and who may touch you in various areas better or for worse.

PG: Wow that is a beautiful question. (Laughter) To be honest with you I am going to have to speak to it and just kind of speak around some issues because I, not that I am afraid of the repercussions, it's just that we do revere these people as elders and they have put themselves on the front line. But, I can say this without feeling like I'm not supposed to speak to it. I think that we are not supposed to speak to it in this kind of format, I'd rather take it to the elder and I don't want to put anyone on blast. But, I have differences with a lot of them. Not only the ones you mentioned but some other ones. And I'm telling you man before too many days go by we are going to have to prepare a table just like this and have the opportunity to question them. For example, I wanted to question Dr. Clarke and his position on why he kept blasting Minister Farrakhan, but, he passed on to the Ancestral realm and I never had a chance to question him. I can question his philosophy and his doctrine now to those people who hold dear to his teachings and discuss it with them. I don't consider myself African. Africa is a land mass, and it's a title, not even created by us as a people as Dr. Ben teaches in his work. We were called Africans by the Greeks. So, I just want to put it out there before I deal with some of these people. Why should I call myself, because I live in Atlanta, am I an Atlantean? Is that not cheap? Okay, let's roll it back a little bit further. I don't vote, should I call myself a Democrat or a Republican? Okay, what other frivolous, d_mn titles. I guess I am in American, should I call myself an American? Am I not deeper than that? So, let's roll it back, let's go further. I am on earth, should I call myself, I don't know...so, you follow where I am going?

TK: Right.

PG: Okay, so, now let's go real deep and then let's go speak to some of these people. If we were to start this interview over and you said, "Well, today we are about to speak to Professor Griff the Minister of Information from the consciously driven rap group Public Enemy." Griff, how you doing today? I would say, "Let's back up, let me introduce myself. I am God having a human experience called Griff." So, if I say that and mean it, and I practice being God everyday as the scriptures teaches we are all Gods, children of the most High God. Are you following me? Why would I cheapen myself and call myself an American, African and all these other titles and labels we put on ourselves. What higher honor can I bestow on this brother, you and these brothers here and when I see the God I greet him as a God? So, all these other labels and titles don't mean anything to me. There are different aspects of me that are on the fringe of what I am but, those things are cheap man. For you to call me African, Dr. John Henry Clarke, is cheap. For you to tell me I am not black, that I am African that doesn't speak to the essence of what I am. I can roll out a timeline and show you in Ancient Kemet and pre-dynastic Kemet, Africa was nowhere in the picture.

Sound: Missile being fired.

PG: We didn't call ourselves African. African is a Johnny come lately new term. For me to be naming myself after a landmass, the whole earth was called Ethiopia and Asia. So, Elijah Muhammad come along and says "No!" We are the Asiatic black man. But, even at the end of that lesson, he said we are Gods of the Universe. Are you following me? So, don't cheapen me man with these..., but that was just a philosophy Dr. John Henry Clark came across with which I totally disagree with. So, let me get to the point. I went on a talk fast. I was just quiet. This is what I borrowed from my father's people who are Native Americans, Blackfoot tribe. They use to go on talk fast for years, just don't talk. I

200

had to go on a talk fast simply because when this Barack Obama thing hit, I said "What is this foolishness?" So, I started hearing the elders I respect say vote for Barack Obama. I said "Stop!" We all know Barack is a puppet in a seat. He is the President of a corporation called America, and they wrote us in as useless eaters. Human resource. He ain't American. We are not citizens of this country because this country is a corporation. You understand what I am saying? I lost a lot of respect for some of these people you mentioned and for some of these other people. So, to hear some of the people you mentioned blasting Minister Farrakhan and other brothers who I do respect. Stop man, stop. So, I don't really have respect for a lot of these people. I love the energy Jewell Pookrim is putting across. Raising the vibration, having us reach for a certain school of thought. You understand what I am saying? Love and respect that man. What Dr. Reverend Phil Valentine is putting out, that's unmatched now-a days. I am still studying his work to the point where I have to reach for that. But I also love what the other brothers that are directly on the front line are doing; Black Dot, True Islam, Brother Sarnetta, that sits right across from the Apollo, Brother Rich and other brothers, Brother Rasheed and some of the brothers that are on the front lines. I'm don't really like what I am seeing on YouTube and some of these other places where we're battling out in a medium that these other people have set up for us to fight one another with these debates and Seti and Brother Aleem and some other people with some stuff that is going on. It's healthy that we do this, in love and we can break bread and show love but to battle one another on YouTube, in this kind of forum and these other people sit back and laugh and say "Ok, that is how they are wasting their time?" Some of the elders I was thoroughly disappointed with to the point where I just had to be quiet man. Be quiet meaning I didn't want to blast them in a public forum. You know, I'd like to see them and discuss why you would...let me mention one of these individuals man so you won't think I am being a punk about this. Anthony Browder, blowing his whole tour, his whole lecture was about voting for Barack Obama. You talking about the same man that gave us the Browder Files, book 1 and 2, The Survival Guide: Ancient Contributions of the Nile Valley Civilization. You know the science of the symbols and you are going to turn around and tell us to vote for Barack Obama? Who is African American, no one said he was a black man, he is not the first black president, and he is an African American as Minister Farrakhan taught us. His father was African, his mother was American. So, he is a true African-American are you following me? So, we need to understand this particular science. It is a shame that people like Anthony Browder has to dumb himself down, reduce himself to that level. He should have been on a tour to teach us the symbolism behind the Presidency of the United States of America. Not have us go and put our names and fill out some form and get our name in that database. It is ugly brother and I don't mean to take up so much time, but I am going to show you the voting machine that Black Dot showed us that they were using to galvanize our people. I can pull it up real quick. I think it is, here it is right here, the voting machine that they used. This is a picture of the voting machine they used, but they call it voter surveillance, you can go to Stealbackyourvote.org. This voting machine takes a picture of you and they send that information of you to security companies and multi-national corporations because it has a built-in recognition software inside of it. Are you following me? It sends out the information to these social service people to know if you are a deadbeat dad. It warns the IRS that we d_mn near have him in our custody, and it pulls up whether you owe student loans, or the IRS. It can tell whether or not you are an illegal alien. It has a hidden camera in it. It has different sensors in it and picks up vibrations in your aura. It knows whether or not you have warrants. Now, they likened President Obama to President Lincoln and President Kennedy so we have to understand why? What happened to both of these Presidents? They got shot in the dome piece right or wrong?

TK: Right, right.

PG: So we need to understand that man. This is real and all of this is part of a three hour lecture I give "The Psychological Covert War on Hip Hop" based on the book I am putting out. So, we have to understand this particular science man, not just my take on it. I can't speak on the body True Islam is calling a lot of these people out. He wants to debate them on his ghetto scholarship.

TK: Okay.

PG: The information that these brothers and sisters are putting out it's critical. You can't read one book and call yourself a scholar and you want to go on the lecture circuit because you read one book.

TK: (Laughter) Right, right. Let's get into subject matter that is taboo to most brothers. Let's talk about our relationships with women, specifically the black woman which will also lead us into the topic of "The Feminization of the Black Male." Even those that are in a the relationship with the woman often face those same dilemmas of the threat of being feminized in relation to what society has taught the black woman in terms of how to treat her man. So, let's talk a little bit about that subject matter and I would like to hear what you would say to other brothers such as myself and even to yourself, you know what I mean?

PG: Right.

TK: How we relate to our women and how they relate to us.

PG: Well, let's look at it this way, I have taught a subject "The Macro and the Micro Womb of the Black Mother Goddess." How many times have I done that lecture Jahi? Once or twice?

JM: At least twice.

PG: Yes, twice where I laid out the information coming from the message of the Most Honorable Elijah Muhammad that taught us and other brothers taught similar science about how we come from the Macro womb of the universe. Elijah Muhammad words it different. He says Allah manifested himself in triple darkness and everything comes from that. This is why it is mandatory we call ourselves black, but that is another story. But, if all of us come from that particular womb, and from that particular source, then the scriptures'

203

reference to womb that bore you and we need to do that. So, when some of the rappers come across with writing derogatory lyrics in reference to the woman oh that's sad. Maybe they don't have this particular science we have and maybe we need to make them aware of this particular thing. So, in educating people I got to put it in such a way where we understand it, not only in an esoteric point of view, hell, but from a surface kind of view. I want to pull something up to read to you that was given to me that could explain that a lot better than I could ever explain it. This was given to me by Professor Smalls and what I did was I went back over the teachings of the Most Honorable Elijah Muhammad and basically, we are talking about the same thing. But, I want to give it to you to the point where, when we go back to listen to this, people can say "okay, I understand what Professor Griff was saying simply because he's dealing with it from an esoteric point of view." Let me pull it up real quick. This goes into the higher science of the Macro and Micro Womb of the Black Mother Goddess. There is a law that is operating in Nature. Let me give you a backdrop. Let's say this brother was Muslim, this brother was Christian, this brother was studying Ifa, and you studying Yoruba and I am studying something else. What I did with religion was ball it up and throw it in the garbage. What I did was I went and looked into higher spirituality concepts and the glue to all of these concepts. So, I started studying the Kabalion, nature. The holy Koran teaches us this that if it be the weight of the atom, and the atom is hidden in the rock and the rock is hidden in the earth yet, Allah will bring it forth. Minister Farrakhan also teaches from the holy Koran that if all the pins were trees and all the seas were ink with seven seas added to them you could not exhaust the words of Allah because all Allah's words are not in a book. It's in the universe. So, I took that, ran with it and looked into it and said "What is Minister Farrakhan saying?" So, I started studying the Kabalion and I noticed that there are laws that are operating in nature that regardless of whether you call yourself a Muslim or a Christian or whatever, we have to abide by. So, I looked at the Law of Correspondence, as above, so below, as within, so without. Is that in the Koran? Yes, because Allah teaches us in the holy Koran to stay on the straight path. Do you understand what I am saying? So, I hung out with Professor Smalls, one weekend in the Caravan to the Ancestors and he gave me this valuable lesson. When you talk about the Law of Correspondence as above, so below, as within, so without whatever you see here in the human body can we see it in the heavens? Because we adorn the heavens. We put the sun, moon and stars up there and we adorn the heavens with stars, and we mapped out the earth in the exact same coordinates. So, you can look into the human body and you can see how we mapped out certain places on the earth because we put it in the heavens. Are you following me?

TK: Yes sir.

PG: So, all we have to do is go back to what the Ancestors taught and stay on the straight path. Did the Ancestors leave us a guide to get back to the God self? Yes. Where did they leave it at? In the Law, the natural law of the universe. So, he says this "You cannot access that deep essence using your enemies pathway to get back to the God self." How am I going to expect him to activate his God consciousness by giving him the bible but don't teach him how to unlock the mathematical code of the bible? Are you following me? So, it says, "You cannot access that deep essence of the God self using your enemies pathway i.e. education, religion, politics." The white man does not know enough about God to know how to get back to God. He says, "He gives you the blueprint, his blueprint, so you can use his blueprint to get you back to the Self." But it never leads you back to the Self; it leads you back to Him. So, in the Lord's prayer that we are made to pray as Christians Our Father which are in heaven, hallow it be thy name, they Kingdom come, Thy will be done. Where? On earth as it is in heaven. As above, so below, as within so without. It is there and they even end the prayer with Amen giving respect and credence to the black God Amen-Ra. You understand what I am saying? So, that is the only way I can answer that and I even put holy Koran and bible scriptures in it to let us know that it is there for us but we are too busy calling ourselves Muslim, Christian fighting and arguing and debating rather than just being Gods and Goddesses. So he gave me this valuable lesson. He says, "I am 48 years old which is my biological, chronological age." He says, "If I have been on the planet for 48 years then I have been collecting data which formulates my consciousness." So, you run into a brother who claims to be conscious, alright, so you are 48 years on the planet, you conscious, fine. He said, "If you do a DNA test on my DNA and put my DNA under the microscope you will find that there are millions of years of history locked up in my DNA that is locked up into me." Only thing you need brother and you need is the method to go back to tap into the millions of years that is trapped inside of you. Then we will know we were kings, queens, goddesses, and scientist. So he says, "If I can look into your cells and find that you were here for millions of years you can only do that if you have had millions of years of genetic wealth and experience that's passed down through you." That means that if you can remember, at least in your subconscious mind, you remember all those experiences that have happened to you throughout all of those millions of years in your consciousness, you can recall those things that you just knew how to tap into your consciousness. You understand what I am saying? He says, "What is the think that gets in the way Professor Griff?" I said, "Shoot, I don't know." He says "All the stuff we have learned in our 48 years called 'consciousness' is getting in the way." Can I prove that? Yes. How many times have you fell into the dream state and you visit places and you meet people while you are dreaming.

TK: Yeah.

PG: We don't even meet these people while we are alive. That is a hint how we can go back into the God self, into the millions of years to figure out who we are. Our consciousness represents and acts as the anti-You. So, you run into this brother on the street and you argue about what Haile Selassie said, what Marcus Garvey said whatever, whatever, okay that is the 48 years you been on the planet. I say this just to sum this up. "You know Professor Griff, there is nothing new under the sun brother." Good, today we are going to go pass the d_mn sun. Then let's go beyond the sun then and let's activate that consciousness.

TK: No doubt (Applause). You talked about why it is important for us to call ourselves black, again, revisiting my previous conversation with KRS1 a very important issue came up. I told them a story about I was driving cross country with an elder and I put on a KRS1 song and the elder immediately told me to shut it off and became very upset and I was like "Why is it that are you upset? This is KRS1." He said, "Well, I heard KRS1 in a lecture with Phil Valentine and say 'I'm not black.'" So, the elder was very offended by that statement. So, I took it straight to Kris and asked them what his position on it was so I would be in a better position to speak in relation to the subject matter. And Kris basically told me that he is evolved pass using black as a political statement towards himself. He is basically in a different place at this time in his life so he doesn't consider himself black. And that also led to an uproar in the room amongst the people who did consider themselves black and felt as though it was very important for us to continue to consider ourselves black. Also stating the fact that KRS1 is one of the main people who taught us to call and consider ourselves black. (Laughter) So, what is your view on the idea of why it is important? You already touched on it, but just elaborate a little. What is your view on the idea of the importance to consider ourselves black?

PG: Alright, I'm smiling because Jahi will tell you I am taking my son through his rites of passage, was that not the lesson today. We dealt with melanin and the question I posed was "What is the essence of blackness?" You know, what makes us black? KRS1 says he is tired of using it as a political statement. It is not political; it is the essence of everything. We are going to say that slow. It is the essence of everything. If you took all the colors and mashed them up in a gumbo you come up with black. So, KRS1 stop. That is child's play that is for third graders. Seriously, okay, now let's get really deep. Melanin is what color?

TK: Black.

PG: You need melanin to do everything. When we woke up this morning and turned on the sun and put it out there so we could have light for the vegetation and so we can grow. Melanin sits in a universe which is black, melanated universe alright? What is your favorite song? Go back in the day. What is your mother's favorite song, or your father's? James Brown? When James Brown first came out with that record was it not on black melanated wax? And resonated with our melanin? And we knew what it was? We didn't need to make up a dance for it, all we did was this. Plain and simple. So, you can have any subject with me and I will take you back to black. Okay, if that is not deep enough for the KRS1's of the world, let's go deeper. "African Cosmology of the Bantu Kongo" written by Fu-Kiau dealing with cosmology. Fu-Kiau gives us this lesson. It says; now remember we are going back to the Micro and Macro Womb of the Black Mother Goddess that is the reason why we cannot escape black. He says, "I am a seed, of a seed of the seed within a seed of a seed of the seed which is energy." So, you already know, you're laughing. You resonated with it already. You know where we are going with this. Okay, I'm a seed, me of a seed, my mom and dad of the seed, the creative force that caused my Mom and Dad to get together. That goes into the science of the sperm and the egg and the chromosomes and that kind of thing which is a kinship to within a seed, which is the universe than of a seed, the dark matter that envelop the universe sits in of the entire seed of energy called matter. If we know that matter and energy cannot be destroyed it is just recreated. What do you mean you ain't black? What do you mean KRS1? You can't escape it. So, let's go back to the long correspondence we dealt with a few minutes ago. As above, so below, as within, so without the same energy, dark matter, womb, and macro womb that the Sun and the planets sit in is the same way we come to birth. What do you mean you are not black? You cannot separate yourself from that which you call God. Anything you try to formulate outside the context of what I just gave you, you're other than that, you are other than

God; you understand what I am saying? You can't separate yourself from everything you call God you are. We are black and what we did we set black in motion and the root to everything, plants, sun sits in black womb. We are in a black universe. Melanin is around us. Melanin lines every organ in your body. Melanin is everywhere. You are black. Everything I can describe about KRS1 is black. The rhythm in which he says his lyrics are black is based on the natural rotation of the universe. The natural pulsation and rhythm of every organ in your body is mathematically coded black. So, what part of you is not black dude? Unless you are on this Humanism stuff, or this New Age stuff that he was on a minute ago. Of course then, you are not black. But, that is somebody else's thing. That is anti-God. That is anti self. You ain't got to tell us we were human, we been knew that. We gave humanity and civilized everyone on the planet and they still haven't caught up. As Jahi tells me all the time Elijah Mohammad said through Minister Farrakhan that we gave them one book out of a warehouse of books.

TK: 60 thousand.

PG: We gave them one book and look what they are doing. Do you understand what I am saying? All those other books are backed up in us so we need to go inside the self. We can do away with this world and create another one. That ain't hard to do.

TK: Indeed.   I studied throughout history let's say starting around the time of Charlie Parker all the way into John Coltrane, Miles. You see commonalities throughout history and dealing with drugs more specifically was heroin which of course we know comes from the poppy seed, the opium plant, and natural resource. After that, came cocaine which we know comes from the cocoa leaf chewed up in Tibet for the sake of energy. Today, amongst the musicians the use of marijuana on levels much greater than at one time, you know what I am saying, in terms of its promotion and its activity and even its marketing as far as the different flavors of wrapping papers and different products and paraphernalia that are coming out surrounding the phenomena. That also being something that originated from a natural resource tobacco and marijuana. What is your view today as far as the generation and the use of marijuana and how it may affect the people because much different than cocaine where you would see the results over a period of time what are some of the pros and cons as far as your views on the use of marijuana?

PG: This answer is going to be about a minute thirty seconds long because I don't smoke weed, never did. I have sat with brothers who have explained to me how the Shamans and the other wise teachers and the Griots and some of the other people tell stories of how we used certain plants for certain things. My father being Blackfoot and Native American use to go in the backyard and pick certain plants, crumble it up, mesh it up, heat some stuff up, drop it in water, wrap his wound with it, put it on his temple, that sort of thing. You know, we can look throughout history and see how we have acted with certain kinds of plants and certain things on the earth as medicine, that particular science we haven't taught these people. Do you understand what I am saying? This brother may light a joint get lifted and be able to astral plane, whereas the next person may light it, get high and wig out. Do you understand what I am saying? That is a deep science man and we haven't taught these people yet. See, that was not in one book that we gave them. (Laughter) That wasn't in that one book. But, I also know on the flip side in this chemical, biological warfare even though he knows it's in you and he knows brothers and sisters use it, he is the Devil now, you have got to keep this in mind, and he wants to benefit from it. "I am going to make the dice and if I catch you using it, I am going to put you in jail." as Malcolm said. I'll make the deck of cards, put it in the store, you buy it, but, if I catch you using it, I'll put you in jail. Do you understand what I am saying? Yeah, he's simply got us bent and to quote a Professor Griff lyric, "It's out there and we use it and we know how to use it." It is a science we haven't taught him. So you see the little medical centers he set up so you've got to get a card signed in order to heal glaucoma and all this stuff. But see, he is on the periphery and the fringes of knowing that particular science on how to turn the hemp into medicine. Do you understand what I am saying? On how to turn the rays of the sun into healing powers when it acts with the melanin, aroma therapy and all these sciences we know that we barely taught him. That is why you find so many of them among us. Do you understand what I am saying? I don't care how broke down the blackman gets from doing whatever, we are still a million dollars. That is why when we greet each other, when we leaving one another we say "Alright, one hundred, I one million" cause we know. We use a high form of alchemy that we haven't taught them that side. We taught them one form of alchemy. We turned metal into gold, or iron or that kind of thing. That is child's play. We use a high form of alchemy because we have melanin that we can turn the sun rays into stored energy and we keep it locked in our body. So we prepare for the winter time so all we have to do during the summer is take two hours of sunlight in a day, so by the time the winter hit if we can come out in a tee shirt, we straight because all we have to do is turn the eternal temperature up, and grow the locks as our antennae. We connect with the universe man. That is nothing for us to do. Child's play.

TK: Amongst doing my research last night I had the opportunity to review some of your previous work; Pawns in the Game, Jail Cell.

PG: Hold it. I want to show something on the screen on how from the Griots morphed into the verbal arts we call it, not the martial arts, but the verbal arts and even using different languages we were able to put together a way of communicating and we have always used plants. We have always used Shamanic where we can fall into a trance like state, a high form of meditation. The Native American do it they beat the drum and get into a trance sort of thing either for one or two purposes to take the evil spirit out or invite the positive spirit to come in. This is how we come up with the dream catchers, that kind of thing we put over the bed. We went through that and we have given birth to what you see the Pastor and the Preacher doing Sunday morning, getting into that trance, raising their hands as you see in

>T

ancient Kemet, the Ka which is the rising of the spirit. So, we've seen that through all the music, the New Orleans Jazz, the Big bands the scattin', the Tango, right on into the Swing and the Beep Bop and Hard Bop and the Rhythm and Blues and Gospel and Urban Blues and Rock and Roll and Soul and free Jazz and Spoken Word, Motown Era and Philly International right up to Hip Hop. We have always had that trance state. You look at some of the Krunk music and you go throughout the South and Memphis and other places where they dance in circles, get into that trance state like the Native Americans use to do, the War dance, Do you understand what I am saying? We have always done that man. That is nothing new, we have always done it and we had the d_mn drug to go along with it. (Laughter) They say Biggie and Jay-Zee use to go into the studio, didn't need pin or paper, tap into the Self and was able to get on the mike and spit. Where is that coming from man?

TK: Right. So now, you have had the opportunity to bless the microphone and work as a musician as well, what I find working as a musician is that I have to find the strength and energy to validate myself. Sometimes, I have to look at my work and appreciate the genius within it and validate it for what it is and then other people come along and understand and validate it. But, if I depend on others to validate it first, often times my music ends up by the way side and it rarely gets any attention. So, I put that energy into myself first. Talk to us a little bit about your previous work, "Pawns in the Game," "Jail Cell" all the way leading up to 7th Octave and what is going on with that and where you stand and where you feel you are as a musician in terms of self validation.

PG: Well, coming though the African American experience at Hass University, headed by and controlled and run by ex-Blank Panthers, myself and Chuck learned African tradition, African language, African Dance, African dress, and that is where we went through our rites of passage. Chuck will tell you the same story. We were young, six or eight, nine coming through these rites of passage. Chuck's mom, very revolutionary sister. So, coming through that, bring you up

212

to date, ended up being DJ Griff in high school, way before the Public Enemy thing, Spectrum City, RC's Music Machine. During that time I was a percussion player, played in a couple of bands. Moved to playing trap set, the traditional drum set. So, I was a drummer. You know the drum is the heartbeat of every song. Coming up to their playing in the band, when I was in the military, as a graduate special military police. Came out of there and hit the scene. Hip Hop was just formulating. Hooked up with a couple of other brothers, went back to the band set, was still DJ Griff coming up out of that, thumbing through the crates. When Hip Hop hit it resonated with me real easy because I was already a drummer. So, when Hip Hop hit, the DJ Griff thing kind of took off and that was when I hooked up with Spectrum City, Bomb Squad, Hank Shockley, Keith Shockley, Jerry Jay, Fat Dre, Ed Luva from MTV from back in the day, and then Chuck D. came on the scene and that morphed into the Public Enemy thing. As an end result of that, I ended up doing a solo projects Pawns in the Game, Chaos to Wisdom, Disturbing the Peace, Blood of the Prophets, The Great Oracle Dialects which is God, Projects, wow, then I did after that And The Word Became Flesh. My poetry Spoken Word album, then I did the 7th Octave album, I did a couple of other side projects; Confrontation Camp, Are Objects in the Mirror Closer than they Appear, some other side projects and I never, ever throughout all of that never asked anyone to validate it. At all. Put the projects out there and people gravitated towards it. It was on them. Never, really heavy promoted this stuff. Whosoever will, as the scriptures say, let them come. That constituted my fan base on an organic tip, cause I never handed anyone a flyer. Roughly, never made any videos of this stuff, you understand what I am saying? I probably have about 10 videos out of 16, 17 projects. Full blown albums you understand what I am saying? So, organically as I put it out there people from all other races and genres of music gravitated towards it. Right now, I am in the middle of the second album, 7th Octave, my rap metal band. It's called God Damage. People say, "So what does God Damage

213

mean?" You know, I have no definition for it; it is whatever you want it to mean. So what is the God damage? What do you think it means? People look at it like, "God Damage. Are you saying 'God D_mn' the music industry?" No man. "Are you saying it is the damage God does?" I'm like no, whatever you want it to mean. However it resonates with you that's what it does. So, I put it out there on an organic tip and whoever gravitates towards it, fine, if you don't cool.

TK: Let's say for example, an artist such as my brother [Data] here would be interested in doing music with you what would be the proper channels or the proper direction he would need to go in terms of getting with you music, or to do songs or something like that.

PG: I would just basically take my e-mail address and my phone number. Before you see what I am doing, let me come and see what you are doing. Rather than you being on something of mine, let's do a fusion. Let's bring part of you and part of me and maybe we can create something different. You understand what I am saying? Let me be on your project and in return, you be on mine. Ain't no real money got to exchange hands, let's just vibe like some of the artist back in the Jazz days. We met at the club and just got down. You bring your instrument, and I will bring mine and see what we can create. You understand what I am saying? Or maybe, we just want to do a PE together where we invite this brother and some other brothers. That is what I am talking about. Why is it that "I got a budget? Come get on. Let me give you a 'G' spit on mine." Stop that man. It ain't about that. We meet in your garage, or your basement and let's do, let's vibe together. I may not be able to light an "L" with you, but we will be able to vibe. You understand what I am saying? So basically, that's all it takes. What I would ask is brothers bring something organic to the table. I don't want to hear what Jay-Zee did, 30 Cent, I mean 50 Cent, Little Weiner, or Little Wayne as they call him, or any of these other people. I don't want to hear what they are doing. Bring you, and surprisingly, Jahi will tell you, I take demo tapes and listen to them. But 99 percent of what I am hearing is somebody else.

TK: Right.

PG: If I want Little Wayne, I will go out and get him, if I want to hear Jay-Zee I will go get him. No, let me hear what you are doing. It ain't a matter of good and bad music, it's what you bringing to the table.

TK: Now, let's say for example, there was an opportunity for a Public Enemy reunion Terminator X, Flava Flav, Chuck, S1W's, Chris...

PG: That would be the second one. We already had that.

TK: Oh really?

PG: Yeah.

TK: So tell me, how did that go? Would you do it again?

PG: Definitely do it again, but it wasn't welcomed. Because, that's when Griff came back to the group and they didn't welcome that. Chuck often said on tour whispering in my ear of course "I don't know how you do it man, I feel it. These brothers hate your guts. Everybody in the group he was talking about, except himself. So, the idea of Terminator coming back was my idea. Having two DJ's on stage like Doug E. Fresh did. DJ Lord and Terminator X, you understand what I am saying? And do a full fledge Public Enemy tour with Terminator X coming back and doing some of the old stuff. All the members in the group blew that out of the water man. Because they don't see vision, they don't see growth. So, that has happened already. But, the second one you just mentioned I spoke about that already. Bringing back the original Bomb Squad, even working with Rick Reuben again, I put it out there already.

TK: So what is Terminator X's position in relation to the group? You know Terminator never spoke. So, give us some insight on where Terminator stood the members of the group.

PG: Terminators still raising ostriches on an ostrich farm, still in North Carolina, still making music but, he still has to mend a personal relationship with Chuck and that, I can't speak on because that is between them two brothers.

TK: No doubt. So before we close I want to backtrack and touch on somewhat of a controversial subject; the relationship that existed between Malcolm and Elijah is something that, amongst my brothers, or some are on one side and some on the other, rarely do they come together on common ground. You know the situation between Malcolm and Elijah even as Farrakhan came up in the movement, and I hear you speak highly of Farrakhan as well. What is your view on Malcolm and how he handled the situation on the news media with Elijah and the Nation bombing his house, the feud between the two and how it all erupted and ended in Malcolm's death?

PG: Well, I can answer that in a nut shell as we close out and say Revolution is not an event, it is a process. I am because we are, so therefore I am. I cannot speak on that and it is ironic that you ask that question because, Jahi, did I not get asked that question today already? This brother wanted to do a whole video thing about it and you know that is going to take a forum. That is going to take having Professor Smalls here, what is your brother's name, Reginald Muhammad teaches a class, Brother Harold. These brothers are experts on this. I'd be speaking from my personal feeling about it, but as Jahi would tell you who travels with me all across the globe, that I speak very highly about Dr. King. Dr. King wasn't no punk man and I think that is one of the things that we need to make known when we talk about the methodology and the ideology and philosophy of Dr. King as opposed to Malcolm X. I see it as one and the same, it's just different methodologies. Different ways of going about it. Do you understand what I am saying? But Dr. King was growing and we seen him growing, Do you understand what I am saying? So, I really can't speak on that. I would do a disservice, and I would be doing you a disservice on whatever medium you plan on putting this out in. Whether you have some brother or sister transcribe this and put this in my brother's forum which is really ill right here. The book, the Young Lion. Whether we do it in this forum or whether we just do it just audio putting it out. We need to do it in all forms. So the young brothers can take this interview right here and put it in a book form and say "Okay, Professor Griff talked about chakras and the aura and being black, here it is on page 36." So, when they go to

216

question KRS1 and Chuck and the rest of these people they can say "Professor Griff, in an interview yada, yada, yada whoop de whop." We need to make small manuals from these interviews like this and make it available to the people.

TK: Absolutely.

PG: Whether your name, his name, my name and whoever. We need to get it out to the people; you understand what I am saying? I can't speak on the Dr. King, Malcolm X issue and do it service. I'd be doing it a disservice, but I can say that we need not get violent with one another, because violence in the context of revolution is not good or evil, it is necessary. Do you understand what I am saying? I am going to quote Dr. King as we end this. He said "Violence is not good or evil, it's necessary. Those that make a peaceful revolution impossible make violent revolution inevitable."

TK: That's life.

PG: That is Dr. Martin Luther King. That ain't Malcolm now, (Laugher) that is Dr. King! Peace, I'm out.

TK: No doubt, no doubt. Real quick. Do you want to let the people know where you might be, what you are doing, where they might catch up with you? Do you have any contact information you want to put out there?

PG: Yes, you can just contact me at: professorgriffpe@gmail.com, or my phone number 678-557-2919. I'm accessible to the people. I am a people person. I am part of the People's Revolutionary Army. Meaning that we are going to formulate an army. We are going to operate, not only on the third dimension, but the fourth, and the fifth dimension dealing with hyper dimensional warfare, as Phil Valentine teaches us to come together to formulate this particular army. I'm accessible, let's build, let's reason, let's break bread, let's talk. The bottom line let's just get free as Dead Prez teaches us.

TK: Absolutely.

LIVE FROM DEATH ROW

Mumia Abu-Jamal's Radio Broadcasts
Copyright 2008 Mumia Abu-Jamal/Prison Radio
Support Professor Griff recorded 2/22/08

Several days ago I received news of a fire which tore through the home and property of the man known as Professor Griff, the more militant member of the legendary hip-hop group, Public Enemy.

While Griff was unharmed (as he wasn't at home at the time), the damage was total. He lost his home, his studio, and everything he owned to the fire, possibly sparked by a gas leak.

As one of the group's most prolific lyricists, Prof. Griff contributed mightily to Public Enemy's sound and messages of black militance, radical resistance and the resurgence of Black history and memory.

Conscious, as ever, he is thankful that is alive.

Millions of people, Black, white, Latino and global, owe their youthful political and social awakening to the throbbing beats, provocative lyrics and moving performances of PE.

In an age when corporate interests have made hip-hop virtually synonymous with mad gangsterism, PE turned on their legions of fans by exhorting them to "Fight the Power!" Their albums, infused with the spirit of Black nationalism and political activism, included works like "It Takes a Nation of Millions to Hold Us Back (1988)." Today, their works are regarded as modern classics of hip hop's true golden age.

Please donate what you can to help this great contributor to one of the planet's greatest bands, and helping to get Prof. Griff back on his feet.

Please contact:
Kavon Shah
P.O. Box 11902
Atlanta, GA 30355

Or touch him on the web at: www.hdqtrz.com. People can donate via PayPal Account.

Griff has spent his time since PE's heyday by lecturing widely on Black and hip hop history.
He shares his experiences and insights with young people, usually for free, considering it his duty to do so.

He really is a professor, for he teaches and lectures on African history, social and political movements, and the like.

In the 1980's and 1990's, Public Enemy provided a glimpse into another side of Black life, strong, conscious, rich with historic imagery, and trying to project something positive into the psyches of the young. Prof. Griff was a central part of that musical and cultural collective.

In this, his hour of need, please let him know that you appreciated his (and his group's) truly positive contribution.

--(c) '08 maj

[Mr. Jamal's recent book features a chapter on the remarkable women who helped build and defend the Black Panther Party: *WE WANT FREEDOM: A Life in the Black Panther Party*, from South End Press (http://www.southendpress.org); Ph. #1-800-533-8478.]

================================

MUMIA'S COLUMNS NEED TO BE PUBLISHED AS BROADLY
AS POSSIBLE TO INSPIRE PROGRESSIVE MOVEMENT AND
HELP CALL ATTENTION TO HIS CASE.

The campaign to kill Mumia is in full swing and we need you to **please** contact as many publications and information outlets as you possibly can to run Mumia's commentaries (on-line and **especially off-line**)!! The only requirements are that you run them *unedited*, with every word including copyright information intact, and send a copy of the publication to Mumia and/or ICFFMAJ.
THANK YOU!!!

SEVENTEEN

Yes Who Can?

THE OBAMA DECEPTION

Professor Griff of the legendary rap group Public Enemy tells the world why he supports Green Party presidential ticket of Cynthia McKinney/Rosa Clemente instead of Barack Obama.

Marcus 3X July 16, 2008

We're here at Nubian Bookstore, Southlake Mall in Morrow and I just bumped into Professor Griff from Public Enemy. Professor Griff, how's it going?

Professor Griff: "It's going all right man, maintaining, maintaining."

Marcus 3X: "Just wanted to get into it real quick. Was on YouTube, a few days ago and saw an M1 from Dead Prez endorse Cynthia McKinney for President of the United States. Just curious as far as if you are supporting Barack Obama or Cynthia McKinney?

Professor Griff: Well from the out start I was never a person to vote at all, man. Not at all. And it really wasn't a tossup between Barack

221

Obama, Cynthia McKinney or that other dude. What's his name? McCain, but a yeah. I didn't vote at all. I never thought about voting because I never thought voting would free us as a people. That's how deep I was going. And then, the last two selections which they call elections never did anything for me. You understand what I'm saying? So when I heard Cynthia McKinney was running after running into M1 in Houston, I just said to myself let me take a look at the Green Party, look at their agenda, see what they're doing. I'm kind of undecided whether I would even vote. But I definitely would endorse Cynthia McKinney what she's doing with Rosa Clemente and reference to the Green Party and running for President, of course.

Marcus Williams: I agree with you on that. I think Cynthia McKinney has proven to be a fighter, especially on issues like election fraud. As we know up in new your city, in primaries in the democratic primaries there are certain parts in Harlem and in New York City where Barack Obama has received zero votes. And then like making that one d_mn comment about receiving no votes. Whereas Cynthia McKinney has always been fighting against election fraud.

Professor Griff: Right, right. You know something. What I think we need to do? Know and understand What is the position of black press, black people in the media who are suppose to be reporting this to black people. I think Chuck D once said that Rap and Hip Hop is the seeing into the black community. You understand what I'm saying? So where are these black reports that are not giving us this information? And if Cynthia McKinney has been on the front lines since day one, and been giving us these issues and the agenda on the table, then how come nobody is reporting this?

Marcus Williams: I agree. There has really been a black media blackout. As far as Cynthia McKinney and Rosa Clemente making history as far as being the first black presidential candidate to be on the ballot in more than 30 something states and as of right now b o is just a presumptive nominee, hasn't nailed it down yet, as the Democratic Party has not had their convention. But we saw this so called 'change candidate' Obama who is highly financed by wall street and big business sign on to the bush FISA deal gave immunity to telecom companies to do wireless I guess warrantless wire taps. What do you think about Barack Obama supporting FISA after saying repeatedly he was against it?

Professor Griff: well this is what I was saying all along. If we don't know the man's agenda and what's on the agenda, FISA, affirmative action, even when it comes to Sean Bell, when it comes to political prisoners, when it comes to a whole myriad of subjects that's suppose to be on the agenda, how come no one is coming to us as a people, not only in the hood, but in the communities how come no one is coming to these conventions to even speak to us about what the agenda is. I'm not surprised about FISA, I'm not surprised about affirmative action, I'm not surprised about what his position on the Sean Bell case and all the other cases. I'm not surprised about his position on reparations and political prisoners; I'm not surprised about Barack Obama. Because a lot of times these things are not trickled down to us the average working person. And we don't know the agenda. No one's reporting the agenda to us. No one is saying ok, When you're talking about a people who don't have access to the information, of course we're going to be left in the dark.

Marcus Williams: Even on the Sean Bell thing the response Barack Obama gave was something to the effect of "expect the verdict." He gave a response even stronger than Hillary Clinton, saying there should be an investigation into it from the Department of Justice. It seems like he has a serious issue as far as wanting to be associated to any black issues of black people in general.

Professor Griff: It seems like he has shied away from galvanizing that black male imaging that is desperately needed to set the situation straight in America. You've seen that with the situation with Jeremiah Wright, you've seen that with Minister Farrakhan. They say he passed the Farrakhan test, but I don't know. I don't think the average white person in America cares. I think those that are in key positions, that control America, I think behind the scenes they care and they're always going to remember. They're always going to care.

But then, let me ask you a question. What was his position on Israel?

Marcus Williams: Actually he went to, he spoke at AIPAC, he actually went to Israel. Spoke at the 60th anniversary of Israel and it was said he pledged 30 billion American tax dollars to continue to fund Israel and even said that attacking Iran is not off the table. Whereas, it was the 40th year anniversary of the MLK assassination and he skipped Memphis! So he can go to AIPAC on their 60th anniversary.......

Professor Griff: You need to say that a little slower. He skipped Memphis! He never even went to Memphis.

Marcus Williams: Yeah, he couldn't be around black people to celebrate the assassination of Dr. King, but he could go to APEC to celebrate the 60th anniversary of Israel's independence.

Professor Griff: So we need to understand and ask the question. Who is Barack Obama? Who is he for real?

Marcus Williams: Yeah. If anybody goes to a website like opensecrets.org, you can pull up all the companies from Wall Street who has been financing Barack Obama. And as you can see there is a big marketing scam with this slogan of change. It's a highly financed operation. I think it's one of the biggest political scams in recent history.

Professor Griff: Did you say www.opensecrets.com?

Marcus Williams: No, opensecrets.org. You can check out all the campaign contributions of all the candidates. And you can see Barack Obama has received more money from Wall Street and big business than any other candidate.

Professor Griff: Wow! So if we just follow the money we can kinda figure out what the agenda is?

Marcus Williams: It's not no d_mn change. I think this change sh_t is one of the biggest political scams in recent history. To see a guy like Barack Obama who lost to Bobby Rush for a congressional seat back in 2000, can resurrect his political career 8 years later, raising d_mn near ½ a billion dollars and people don't ask the question, "where did this dude come from?"

Professor Griff: Then we need to ask ourselves, "Who is the Zbigniew Brzezinski in the grand chess board? We need to ask who these people are who openly came out and supported Barack Obama? But we're not doing the research. We're not doing the investigative reporting and getting this information to our people.

Marcus Williams: And then in the democratic primaries, the whole issue of no hiring was about NAFTA and then in the primaries he was trying to portray the image that he was against NAFTA. Then we find out during the process most recently that his economic advisor, Allen Gulsby, is a member of skull and bones, which John Kerry and George Bush are members of, told a consulate in Canada that 'wink, wink' Barack Obama is just talking. Don't pay the rhetoric no attention. He's pro NAFTA. We see Barack Obama flip flopping on NAFTA, FISA. Even most recently in the New York Opt Ed, he said we must send 10,000 more troops to Afghanistan. So what do you think about all these major flip flops on this so called change candidate, Obama?

Professor Griff: Notice the language, man. The whole flip flopping language is the same flip flop language they used on John Kerry. And John Kerry later found out he was a part of the whole scheme. John Kerry and George Bush are both members of the skull and bones. I think that b o has been given a pass by the blue bloods. He has been given the ok by certain secret societies for them to let him in. I truly believe imperialism and fascism need a face lift. And that face lift is going to have to be black. And the reason why I believe that is simply because their trying to go into Africa. Well they are already in Africa but they want to control all the natural minerals their going to need to carry themselves into the 21st, 22nd, 23rd centuries. You follow me? They have to go through a phase galvanizing the masses of dark skinned people that truly believe

225

change needs to come. But the change that they're talking about is not necessarily a change for the better for the masses of dark skinned people. But it's not a change for us, the little people man on the totem pole.

Marcus Williams: what do you think about the technique Obama's handlers have used as far as, you know, the repetition of change, change, change? What do you think about that whole technique they are using in the field?

Professor Griff: Well, repetition is the mother of learning. We have to understand that. If you teach a lie over and over and over again, surely, later on if you hear it enough, it becomes the truth to some people. Because of you don't have the ability to go beyond and underneath the lie to undo the lie. Do you understand what I'm saying? We get a lot of our news from the media. You understand what I'm saying? How you gone believe FOX? How you gone believe CNN?

Marcus Williams: Right. Yeah it's a like their using the whole little Messiah type thing. The marketing scheme used to blow up Barack Obama, it's ingenious he's the product. Change is the slogan. No substance.

Professor Griff: The marketing and mind control. No one looks at the agenda. As long as he positions himself right, have the right tie on, have the right smile, repeat the slogan over and over, repeats it and drives it home the average American is just going to swallow it hook line and sinker, and we don't even know what the agenda is.

Marcus Williams: Since your being in the music industry and the hip hop industry, what do you think about the artists like Jay Zee, P Diddy, 50 Cent, Kia whoever, all these artists endorsing Barack Obama? What do you think about all these hip hop heads? Is it like American idol, just a fad to endorse Obama without doing their homework and see what he's doing?

Professor Griff: I think it's stroking the master, like getting your head stroked by the master, like lap dogs. You've done a good days work and the master strokes them and sends them on back to the d_mn doghouse. I think in most cases people like P Diddy, Jay Z, and a lot of these cats don't have any political awareness anywhere. If it doesn't benefit them financially, their not really politically astute to the point where they can be very open and honest and candid with us as black men and black women to say okay, "tell us what they really think.... the camera is not on now, you're not in the studio, you're not on stage, tell us what you really think?" And if what you really think does not go hand in hand with what you're telling the people that love honor and respect you and support you then what's really your agenda? You understand what I'm saying? Jay zee already knows the handshakes, he's already taken the oath; they already let P Diddy in You don't get to the 20 million dollar club without getting these peoples stamp of approval. P Diddy already had the Vote or Die campaign which is utterly stupid, and ridiculous and idiotic for a Negro like that to be giving you that kind of ultimatum you either vote or you die. Jay Z openly supports Barack Obama, 50 Cent openly supports Hilary Clinton...

Marcus Williams: I think he changed his position. 50 Cent is now supporting Barack Obama.

Professor Griff: Okay but that would be a smart move to do that. Because now you have to be or appear to be politically astute cause you don't want to lose that particular clout. You understand what I'm saying. They have to appear politically astute so they can be called on by their handlers, by their white handlers. See, Puffy tried to appear neutral, Vote or die, galvanizing all that young energy, that demographic between 18-35 demographic, get them out to vote, get them registered; come to find out that all those names when your register to vote all those names go into the database for the selective service draft. And this they're not telling us. No one is saying this is the electoral process and this is how it works to educate us about voting. They are just saying come register, and at that time they wanted us to vote for Bush or Kerry and both of them are cousins, and both of them belong to skull and bones.

Marcus Williams: Yeah, I mean that just really hurt me to see some conscious rappers some consider like Mos Def and Common supporting Barack Obama. Are there any other conscious hip hop artists like yourself and M1 from Dead Prez that are supporting Cynthia McKinney?

Professor Griff: Well, I reached out to NY Oil who came to do a fundraiser, UNO from Boston, what's his name; Immortal Technique is coming to town. I tried to reach out to Gene Gray; other rap artists who are out there on the front lines and not afraid to speak. I called Tom Morello from Rage Against the Machine, to have that conversation with him; Stick Man from Dead Prez and some other people. But this is new. It just hit the press that Rosa Clemente is going to be the vice president on the green party ticket under Cynthia McKinney running for president on the green party ticket. So I'm waiting to hear back from a couple of these people I have yet to speak with Chuck D. I will see him this Friday in Chicago. I even want to ask Flava. A lot of these people got the Flava-ism going on; they want to be a Flava-tron, so I want to see the Flava Flave hypnotic magnet going so I want to hear what they have to say. I want to see what Flava has to say. Because this is not new. We went through this same thing with Jesse Jackson, everybody picking and choosing sides. You understand what I'm saying? But the agenda is not being laid out this time and I want to see what people have to say. Are we going to follow someone blindly because they look like us? Or are we going to dig into the agenda and see what we are actually going to be getting at the end of the day.

Marcus Williams: Remember at the end of the day Cynthia McKinney has proven, when compared to Barack Obama, you can't even compare them. Cynthia McKinney is out front fighting against Bush on issues like 9-11, what they knew about 9-11, and election fraud. There are so many issues down the list that I know of where Cynthia McKinney has proven to be worthy of support. I just really think it's so sickening that so many people are falling for Barack Obama, especially a lot of black people, when there is somebody like Cynthia McKinney who has been proven to be worthy of support.

Professor Griff: Without a shadow of a doubt! But you know something, I think a lot of the people who are supporting Barack

Obama want to see change; they just don't want to dive into the issues. Cynthia McKinney is dealing with the issues. A lot of time we don't want to know the issue. We don't want to know the issue. We feel, what do you call this thing when you get this false sense of gratification but because a black man is in office everything is going to be all right. No, everything is not going to be all right. Not until we look into the agenda; what the democratic has been about, is about, and will be about, regardless of whether Barack Obama is the president or not, and that's real. Because we got deceived under Bill Clinton. We thought he was the first black president and everything was cool, just because he played the saxophone, smoked some weed, and got some head in the White House. And we can't be deceived like that anymore. Then he moved to Harlem, and we thought it was a wrap, we thought it was ballgame, you understand what I'm Saying? And that's not cool. You understand what I'm saying? And we can't be deceived and tricked this time.

Marcus Williams: Right, right. So in closing can you give a final sentence why people should support and donate money to the Cynthia McKinney campaign?

Professor Griff: I think simply because in a nutshell if you want a candidate if you want a president who is going to put the issues on the table, that's going to resolve the old issues, that's going to bring up the issues and really deal with what we're really being faced with not only in America but on the global scene, I think we really need to put our energy, our resources, and our money behind Cynthia McKinney for president of the united states on the green party ticket, with Rosa Clemente as vice president. And this is coming from Professor Griff, under the Minister of Information of Public Enemy, still of Public Enemy, and probably an enemy with inside Public Enemy. But nonetheless, that's what I think we need to do, if you believe in the voting process as all.

Marcus Williams: I really appreciate you

Yeah man. Give thanks man. Just coming through the store, picking up some information so I can become astute as to what I'm dealing with as far as politics. And politics is the science of governing people and we need to understand that.

Marcus Williams: Well, thanks man. Hopefully more people such as yourself will come and help us out. Roseanne Barr is supporting Cynthia McKinney; more people like Danny Glover, Harry Belafonte and others need to come out and endorse Cynthia McKinney because this Barack Obama hysteria, this scam needs to be put down.

Professor Griff: **Give thanks man. Cynthia McKinney do your thang! I'm here**

EIGHT

Know The Ledge

Occult Science Radio July 2009 Parts 1, 2 & 3
Brother Curtis – Moderator (BC)
Professor Griff-Guest Speaker (PG)

BC: You have been up in the industry as an active participant; ok, world tours, a million hours in the studio the whole nine yards. Ok...you are talking from the inside, not somebody from the outside how did we go from the type of hip-hop, that "Throw your hands up in the air, everybody have a good time to brothers shooting each other down in the street to smacking up the sisters?

PG: I think we can go back and we can look at let me see how far do I need to go back to adequately answer that question? I think we can go back recently and pick up a book entitled "The First Millennium edition of the American Directory of Certified Uncle Toms." On page 236 it talks about the nefarious niggerization of rap music. Let me pull it up. It says "The Uncle Toms that haunt the middle echelons of the music business had the first opportunity to nurture and develop the new, original sound emerging from their own use. Talking about black people. Alright? These Uncle Toms were there, they heard Hip-Hop. They could have nurtured it and morphed it into something, but instead, they rejected it. The whole movement, they rejected it. As strongly as the youth embraced it, they rejected it. They ignored urban appeal, and true to all middle class acculturation, sought their talent from artists whose styles were of the Lionel Ritchie, Michael Jackson cross over type. White people rejected it? No, whites latched on to it you understand what I am saying? And then young whites seen Public Enemy coming, they gave birth to Grand Nubian, righteous teaching, Buster Rhymes and other people, Queen Latifah, the other groups, and then they decided with Quincy Jones's Vibe magazine and other people that they had propped up to niggerize Hip-Hop and other rap music. They made it very profitable to call yourself a nigger. So, when they started paying people like NWA, because NWA are victims of this also, but they started paying people like NWA to propagate and to promote this nefarious niggerization, it made it cool for every group that came after NWA to model and pattern themselves after NWA . So it is fashionable and cool to call yourself a nigger now. Now this is not Griff, this is on page 236 of this First Millennium addition of the American Directory of Certified Uncle Toms. And it also says that the negro child will begin it with an humiliating picture of the negro as dirty, shiftless, lazy, happy-go-lucky, smelly, ignorant, treacherous, superstitious and cowardly and he may find himself expected to live up to this.

BC: Sounds like the Willie Lynch papers.

PG: Exactly, all over again. And we are revisited that with Hip-Hop. So they used Quincy Jones' magazine, Vibe magazine and they still do. They used NWA so while Lyle Cohen and Jimmie Ivine were getting rich creating this East coast West coast beef Tupac and Biggie were being shot down like dogs and animals in the street. So we have to address that. Are you following me?

BC: Yes, sir.

PG: And that is real, so John Potash put together the book "The FBI War on Tupac Shakur and Black Leaders" and he connected the dots. Now this is a white dude putting this out. He connected the dots to show you there is an attack on black leaders and young, Black, rap artist were the new, young Black leaders. Like Fela Kuti said, "Music is a weapon" and they know that. Are you following me?

BC: Yes sir

232

PG: So inside of the book "Behold the Pale Horse" by William Cooper, whom by the way, they murdered.

BC: Straight up, on a parking ticket.

PG: Thank you. So in his book "Behold the Pale Horse" written by William Cooper a former naval intelligence officer in regards to a document concerning the American public, it states, "...diversion is the primary strategy." The simplest method for securing silent weapons and gaining control of the public is to keep the public undisciplined and ignorant of basic system principles while keeping them confused. And this is what these reality shows are doing. Confused about gender, confused about political issues, confused about your role, confused about religion, confused about politics. It says, "Keep them confused with matters of no real importance." Whereas the media, m-e-d-i-a which stands for Multi-Ethnic Destruction In America are main that European devil of action keeps the adult population attention diverted from real social issues and captivated by matters of no real importance. It goes on to say the schools keep the young ignorant of mathematics, real economics, real law and real history. Entertainment is kept below the six grade level. When you start hearing songs like "Laffy-Taffy" and these kinds of songs will hit your lower chakra and vibrate that negative energy, activating your pituitary gland activating those hormones. Now you've got grown ass men making songs for 12 year olds.

BC: Teach brother.

PG: i.e. Jay-Z. So the public is kept busy working, and the adult has no time to think and that is exactly what they produced and they wrote about it inside of a book called "The Tavistock Institute of Human Relations: Shaping the Moral, Spiritual, Cultural, Political and Economical Decline of the United States of America" by John Coleman. Now John Coleman is the gentleman that wrote "The Committee 300" and "The Committee 300" is that organization that gets together to decide what the trends are going to be in the black community. So, when you see people wearing Mohawks and tight pants and wearing earrings and acting like women that was manufactured and put among us.

233

BC: Teach brother.

PG: So we have got to understand that and how they did it. It says they devised a system and the aim of the 12 tonal system that they devised shortly by British Intelligence operatives from Tavistock Institute in England. They put these 12 tones among us and created this thing, Punk Rock and this other uncontrollable music, look up "Operation Paper Clip" and it will tell you all about it. But Ordonal was a system of music that could program the mass music culture capable of eroding the morals of its listeners until they decline to a point where they will totally be degraded by it. And that is what is going on today. The music is bringing us down to an animalistic level to a point we don't even care about the art form, we just want a paycheck. So now it's cool for a Jim Jones to come out talking about "Na na na na na" and grown folks go for it. You understand what I am saying? It's cool for these cats to come out with songs talking about "I'm Stupid," "You're Stupid," "We Stupid." Why does that appeal to grown men and grown women and it shouldn't. We have **to understand that man.**

BC: That is right. I mean basically once back in the '80's, I mean once when I saw and I don't say this to flatter you, but I remember things when they started way back, when I saw what the Industry..., how they began to obstruct Public Enemy and you went down for a minute, that is when I basically lost interest, brother. I mean I am "Old School" anyway, I'm an Earth Wind and Fire man, I'm a "Kool and The Gang" man, ok so now when I heard Public Enemy back in the day, I said "OK, this is what I am talking about" and then we know what happened, ok?' So, after that went down, I basically lost interest.

PG: Yes, because they used NWA to neutralize Public Enemy. You know what I am saying? Unbeknownst to NWA they didn't know, they were victims of this.

BC: Black Dot said the same thing.

PG: So we have to understand that particular dynamic. Our young parents out there are unaware that these people themselves, Joel Bakan put out a DVD called "The Corporation," he said, "Children, as tomorrows consumers

234

represent a huge market today and therefore are fair game." So they are attacking the children using tones and frequencies, and parents, who want to see our children happy, we go out and use our credit cards, our hard earned dollars to make sure our children are happy. So we get the new sneaker and the new video games and the new songs that come out this kind of thing thinking we are making our children happy. We are feeding our children's mind and soul to the wolves.

BC: Teach brother.

PG: But when I break this down, I get more enemies than I ever get friends, but I am cool with that so know that with Black Dot, Valentine, yourself and other people I am in good company.

BC: Thank you brother, I am honored by that. One thing I know is that when you are a light bringer, you are going to have enemies, but see, when you are a light bringer, ok, the Universe is on your side, and see all your haters eventually will fall. As long as you keep doing you and doing your thing and uplifting the fans ain't nothing going to happen.

PG: Right, exactly. There were no brothers attempted to get together to create their own black distribution company. Oh, that's when the Hip-Hop cops, that is when the dossier file was created, 500 pages thick. If you watch the DVD "Rap Sheets," that is when the Hip-Hop task force was created and they started doing surveillance on the rappers. There were four individuals that we need to take notes and notice to whom they put under their surveillance and they sought to destroy these brothers. Now, I'm not particularly cool with some of these brothers lifestyle, but none the less, they are my brothers. We have to look at Dame Dash, we have to look at Suge Knight, we have to look at Irv Gotti, and we have to look at Jay Prince. These four gentlemen got together and was going to put up 30 million dollars apiece to get and create their own distribution company to distribute black music. These people got together and said "We will never let it happen. It will happen over out dead bodies. All in one week, I am going to tell you the short version of this story. All in one week they raided the offices of these four brothers. I am going to say them again; Damon Dash, Suge Knight, Irv Gotti and H Prince out of Texas. The FBI raided their offices and confiscated their records and started piecing cases against these brothers. And you know Dame Dash's situation, he is back with Jay-Z, after they took Roc-A-Fella from him, made Jay-Z the President, bought it for 7 million I think, turned around and sold it for 270 million and they moved him right on out of the picture. And now, I heard through the African grapevine that he is back with Jay-Z broke. Suge Knight, you already know his story. You understand he went through some court cases and end up having the Jewish woman, the owner now of everything Death Row put out. I think she bought it for 22 million dollars, no 25 million. Ain't that something! Bought the entire catalog. I am going to have to get this woman's name so I can put it in my records. Irv Gotti, him and his brother were brought up on charges, remember, a couple of years ago?

BC: Oh yeah!

PG: And it was publicized because they raided his offices and tried to connect him to some mob ties and some drug dealing and that kind of thing thanks to your man 50 Cents. We will talk about that in a minute. Then Rap-A-Lot owner, H. Prince who they connected to embezzling money and fraud and laundering money, but Jay-Z was privy to this information and Jay-Z was one of the ones that took it back to them. So what they did they do, they bought Jay-Z off to tell the short version of the story and each one of these individuals had to make a blood sacrifice. So, let's take a closer look at this. Who did Dame Dash sacrifice? He sacrificed his fiancée who he was engaged to at the time, Aliyah who died in a plane crash. Who did Suge Knight sacrifice, Tupac. Who Irv Gotti was suppose to sacrifice, but it didn't happen, Ashanti. She broke away from the camp and now she is doing well. But that was his blood sacrifice. Are you following me?

BC: Yes sir, teach.

PG: So H. Prince was heard through the African grapevine that he had inked a deal with the brother Pimp C, and if you can remember, Pimp C would lie before he died and he started blasting people calling people homosexual and this kind of thing and he was calling people out and shortly after they they found him dead in a hotel from an overdose. Would you want to operate in that 20 million dollar club and higher, the 100 million dollar club where these brothers were operating in, oh you have to pay the price. You have got to bond yourself to these people forever. Let's look at some of the other people that have bonded themselves to this demonic energy. Michael Jordon, who did he lose? His dad. Bill Cosby, who did he lose?

BC: His son.

PG: I could go on and on. When Kanye West wanted to be up in that space so bad, he took the oath, and signed on, became a Mason, and took the oath, then did Lucifer, Son of the morning, for Jay-Z and that was his initiation and sure enough, he lost his mom. Jennifer Hudson wanted to be up in that space. Yes, her family got taken out on some ritual killings, are you following me? We need to understand this particular thing, you are not going to operate up into the 50, 100 million dollar club and you not pay the ultimate price now, not the ultimate price, but make a blood sacrifice. Jay-Z was well aware of all of this, so they paid him off. How did they pay him off, they gave him Roc-A-Wear, they gave him Roc-A-Fella records, Roc Nation, Jay-Z Inc, then the New Jersey Nets, he owned a part of that. J Hotels, 40-40 Club, I can go on and on bro, and this is happening right before our eyes. They Niggerized the music and soon as Jay-Z was made President of Def Jam, guess who he signed? Two known drug dealers, Young Jeezy and Rick Ross who would perpetuate and carry on the madness and the negative demonic frequency. Are you following me?

BC: Yes sir,

PG: We need to understand that to this degree. Now, we love these brothers, but they are victims of a diabolical plan to take Hip-Hop off course and they're successful. Hip-Hop is no longer the voice of the voiceless. We have to understand that man.

237

BC: Corporate. I almost didn't want to take it because you were dropping it so heavy, but we have to honor the fans.

Caller: What can brothers do that are ready to end this madness?

PG: I think what we need to do is take bits and parts of information, like when I was coming up. I took bits and parts of information and said to myself "I'm holding on to every bit of information I get and I'm staying on a straight path and I am not deviating from it, not at all. So, at the end of the day I can say, "Nope, I didn't harm my brother, I didn't rob anybody, I didn't steal from nobody, I didn't shoot anybody in the head, I didn't deceive anyone." But then, what did I do that was good? Ok, I stayed away from those things, but what did I do on the flip side that was good? Did I help somebody in need? Did I feed the people on the spiritual level? What did I do and at the end of the day, we have got to say, "Did I do my part?" People come to me all the time "Yo Griff is this sh_t ever going to change man?" So, I say, "Well, what did you do to bring about the change?" You did your part bro, I'm doing my part, we have got to encourage other people to do their part. Everybody has a job in this.

Caller: I understand what you are saying. But dudes ain't doing nothing about it. When you got brothers trying to speak up for people and dudes that say they care, and dudes that are saying things about certain people, you can't even say you can deal with your own problems the same anymore. You have shown that your brother is killing you on a higher level and we are dancing to that frequency. The frequency has got to change and I am telling you as a man I am with you. There are a lot of brothers who are with you, but it is all about how we going to move. Why talk, if you are not putting in any action, I don't want to hear your whole speech. I don't want to talk no more. What are we doing? Let's get it. I want to know I left this earth doing the right thing. If I have to shed blood, so be it!

PG: You are absolutely right brother, 1000 percent but my thing is this all I need to do is link with about a thousand brothers just like you, we could set it! I want to be with like-minded spirits. I love your spirit. My man told me today, we have to use money as a means to an end. Not the end. Money is not the end. We have to define what the end is and what do we want? And it has been laid out by all these leaders that came before us. We cannot let all these leaders that sacrificed their lives and put it down for us just go.

* *

Completed Works
Professor Griff

1990 Pawns in the Game

1991 Kao's II Wiz-7-Dome

1992 Disturb N Tha Peace

1994/95 G.O.D. Gryt Orcle Dlyctz (never released)

1998 Blood of the Profit

(2000) Confrontation Camp Griff recorded the album "Objects in the Mirror May be Closer than they Appear" with his group

2001 And the Word Became Flesh

2002 the DVD "911 is a joke" the Un-Holy war on Terrorism

2002 The DVD 'Hip-Hop and Revolution"

2003 "Mentacide "A global Mis-education", "A Higher form of killing"

2003 Strange love "Has public enemy lost its flavor"

2004 book Atlanta Musick Biz (R.I.P Resource Information Publication)

2004. 7th Octave he recorded the album "The Seventh Degree"

2007 Films: "Turntables" and "The Chip Factor"

2007 " *The Psychological Covert war on Hip Hop*" (DVD/Book)

2008 "Turn off Channel Zero."

2008 DVD The Metaphysical God-des-stry of the soul of Hip-Hop

2009 Beyond The Psycho-*Covert War on Hip Hop.*

Professor Griff Info: professorgriff@hdqtrz.com (678) 557-2919
professorgriffpe@gmail.com

Analytixz is an in depth analysis into 20 years of conversation and enter-views with Public Enemy's Minister of Information.

Learn from 20 years of information that has helped to shape and mold the hip-hop history. Read first hand from the Professor himself.

Paperback; 254 pages; $19.95
ISBN: 978-0977124-2-1-3

BOOK TITLE	QUANTITY	PRICE

PAYMENT INFORMATION: Check One

_____VISA _____MC

_____CHECK _____MONEY ORDER _____CASH

Please mail payment to: Heirs to Shah
P.O. Box 11902, Atlanta GA 30355

Shipping & Handling	
Tax	
Total	